SOUL
FOOD
ADVISOR

The Southern Table

Cynthia LeJeune Nobles, *Series Editor*

SOUL FOOD ADVISOR

RECIPES and TIPS for AUTHENTIC SOUTHERN COOKING

•••••••••••••••••••••

CASSANDRA HARRELL

LOUISIANA STATE UNIVERSITY PRESS • Baton Rouge

Published with the assistance of the Borne Fund
Published by Louisiana State University Press
Copyright © 2016 by Louisiana State University Press
All rights reserved
Manufactured in the United States of America
FIRST PRINTING

DESIGNER: *Mandy McDonald Scallan*
TYPEFACE: *Livory*
PRINTER AND BINDER: *Maple Press, Inc.*

All photographs are courtesy Cynthia LeJeune Nobles.

Library of Congress Cataloging-in-Publication Data
Names: Harrell, Cassandra, 1953– author.
Title: Soul food advisor : recipes and tips for authentic southern cooking/
    Cassandra Harrell.
Description: Baton Rouge : Louisiana State University Press, [2016] | Series:
    The southern table | Includes bibliographical references and index.
Identifiers: LCCN 2016008108| ISBN 978-0-8071-6376-4 (cloth : alk. paper) | ISBN
    978-0-8071-6377-1 (pdf) | ISBN 978-0-8071-6378-8 (epub) | ISBN 978-0-8071-6379-5 (mobi)
Subjects: LCSH: African American cooking. | Cooking, American—Southern
    style. | LCGFT: Cookbooks.
Classification: LCC TX715.2.A47 H37 2016 | DDC 641.5975—dc23
LC record available at https:lccn.loc.gov/2016008108

The paper in this book meets the guidelines for permanence and durability of the Committee
on Production Guidelines for Book Longevity of the Council on Library Resources. ∞

In loving memory of my sister,
Debra Y. Simmons

CONTENTS

(Photos appear after page 124)

ACKNOWLEDGMENTS

Many thanks to . . .

My good friend Carolyn Conley for allowing me to include her mother Elnora's Sweet Milk and Jelly Cake recipe. I grew up eating this wonderful dessert, and I would not take anything for the memories this cake still brings. Thanks, Carolyn, for sharing this special treat.

My husband, Earl, the greatest barbecue chef in the galaxy, and an expert on smoking meat. He gave me encouragement and support throughout this project, and I am especially grateful to him for letting me use his fantastic barbecue and meat-smoking recipes.

SOUL
FOOD
ADVISOR

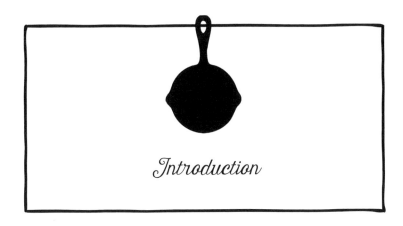

Introduction

I've never considered myself a fancy chef. Instead, I am a proud home cook who grew up in a little town called Halls in southwest Tennessee, and I've been standing in front of a stove for more than forty years. A decade of that time was spent working at the catering business I operated with my husband, Earl, in Milwaukee, where customers raved about dishes I consider common, such as corn bread and greens. And those folks in Wisconsin kept coming back again and again. To my surprise, our style of soulful southern cooking became so popular up there that we soon found ourselves cooking for the NBA's Milwaukee Bucks, and we even received an award for our efforts from the U.S. Department of Commerce.

MY DEEP SOUTHERN ROOTS

Presently, I live about forty-five miles southeast of Halls in Jackson, Tennessee, where our main industries are manufacturing, tourism, and agriculture. And as in any self-respecting southern town, the food here revolves around the tomatoes, cucumbers, onions, and greens that many of us, including me, grow in our own backyards. Yes, we are particularly fond of corn bread, pork, smothered greens, biscuits, and scratch cakes. We still carry casseroles to new or sick neighbors and to funerals, and we invite the preacher over for Sunday roast. And don't forget about barbecue, by far our most popular regional food, and a specialty of our nation's barbecue city, Memphis, which is only a few hours away.

The stews, roasts, vegetables, breads, pies, and cakes that come out of my kitchen are traditional southern soul food, as some call it, and they are greatly influenced by my grandmother, my aunts, and my mother, the women who taught me how to cook. I've also picked up hints from Earl, the world's greatest barbecue chef. So this book honors them for their part in handing down my family's historic recipes and for the innovative recipes they created.

It was pretty much impossible to grow up in Halls without learning how to cook. The 2,300 or so wonderful people in this close-knit community all love life and their families, and they also enjoy eating the region's traditional foods.

My hardworking parents were Emerson and Mamie Taylor. In my childhood, we lived with my grandmother, Big Mama (also named Mamie), the originator of many of my recipes. Our three-bedroom house was in the middle of town, and our neighborhood consisted mostly of family and good friends. Even though we were close to grocery stores, Big Mama had a huge garden on the side of her house where she grew tomatoes, green cabbage, garden onions, peas, butter beans, greens, and beets. She also had pecan trees, and she grew peaches; just imagine the home-cooked goodness that came out of her kitchen!

The rest of my food-loving family includes my sister Dawn, and two brothers, Deverick and Dwayne. My son, Travis, has turned out to be a fine cook, having picked up a few of our family's culinary secrets along the way. Finally, there's my older sister, Debra, who passed away a few years ago. She was my rock, and she loved cooking as much as I do.

My ancestors hail from Tennessee, Kentucky, and Missouri, and the original recipes they passed down reflect the food of those regions. And these scattered relatives, like me, learned cooking by observing each other in the kitchen. Years ago, African American cooks didn't have cookbooks, and my family didn't either. I listened to cooking stories from my mother, who listened to cooking stories from my grandmother. Who knows how far back these recipes go? But I do know that the verbal handing down of cooking techniques is the reason why I and so many African Americans can cook without a recipe. We simply remembered main ingredients and then added our own special touches. And even though we certainly use cookbooks today, we can still tell by color when a cake is done, and we know by feel when a stirred pot of beans is tender and ready.

My longest cooking memory goes back to when I was about four, when I used to crawl up in a kitchen chair and watch Big Mama fry hot-water corn bread in a cast-iron skillet on her old electric stove. Even though I wasn't old enough to cook, that's when I first grew interested in cooking.

THE MILWAUKEE CONNECTION

Our catering business started in 1994, when Debra was living in Milwaukee and Earl and I joined her and brought along our southern flair for food. I found my niche as a caterer after I helped a friend in Wisconsin prepare food for the homeless in a local shelter. This experience was so rewarding—especially seeing the grateful, smiling faces when the food arrived. Even after Earl and I started our catering business, I still found time to make my way to the shelter.

We stayed in Wisconsin ten years and returned to Tennessee after Debra had moved back and gotten sick and needed our care. But during that time in Milwaukee, we owned and operated a barbecue restaurant called Earl's Southern Bar-B-Que, along with a catering company called Earl's Southern Catering. We specialized in southern cuisine because that's what we knew. As I mentioned, we were a huge hit, and our menu was the talk of that big midwestern town.

Aside from a catering contract with the NBA's Milwaukee Bucks, we also cooked for sporting events and national trade shows at Milwaukee's Midwest Convention Center. To top all that, the U.S. Department of Commerce honored us with its 2000 Midwest Regional Service Firm of the Year Award for best catering services, and we received the 2003 Harvest of Hope Award from the Milwaukee Center for Teaching Entrepreneurship.

MY PARTNER IN BUSINESS AND LIFE

A big part of our business success came from Earl's barbecue. And, I must say, when it comes to Earl I burst with pride. He's a self-taught barbecue chef who is tops in his field, despite having a severe disability. In 1982 his hand was severed in an industrial accident, and it was replanted after twelve hours of surgery. That accident still occasionally causes Earl a little suffering, but that doesn't stop him from preparing delicious smoked barbecue that he smothers with his secret sauce.

A few of Earl's recipes are included in this book, and he has also helped me coauthor a few other cookbooks I want to tell you about: *Soul Food Lovers' Cookbook: A Treasured Collection from Three Generations of Southern Cooks* and *Unforgettable Appetizers: Memorable Recipes for Any Occasion* (both available on soul-food-advisor.com). There's also *How to Be Your Own Best Cook* (available as an e-book on soul-food-advisor.com). We've also written the following books that relate to Earl's accident: *Give This Man a Hand: A True Story of Losing a Hand and Regaining It* and *Surviving in the Workplace: An Industrial Workplace Survival Guide.*

WHAT'S THE DIFFERENCE BETWEEN SOUL FOOD AND SOUTHERN FOOD?

All soul food is southern food, but not all southern food is soul food. Let me explain: The cuisine referred to as "soul food" originated in the kitchens of African American slaves in the late 1800s. In the mid-1960s, southern-style cooking by black Americans was renamed "soul food" in honor of the black cooks who prepared food during the era of slavery. It was also a reminder that these cooks paved the way in the development of a distinct African American cuisine.

In the beginning, soul food recipes typically called for ingredients indigenous to Africa, and they referred to dishes that were often cooked on American plantations. In contrast, modern soul food is mostly known as southern or comfort food, and for many families it's the dishes that bring back memories of special dinners and celebrations.

So the main difference between soul food and southern food is basically that soul food was prepared by African American cooks during the days of slavery. These are also the dishes that were popular in the succeeding African American culture, such as fried chicken, barbecue and grilled meats, hoecakes and a variety of corn breads, sweet potato dishes, collard greens and black-eyed peas, and homemade country cakes, to name a few. Many of these foods also satisfy the definition of a traditional southern meal. Just remember that soul food's beginnings were on plantations, and that these dishes were created by folks who didn't have many ingredients to work with.

WHY SOUL FOOD ADVISOR?

I titled my website Soul-Food-Advisor.com because I've been cooking soul food—or southern food, if you'd like—all my life and because I've taught many a youngster my cooking techniques. And that title just naturally carried over to this book. So I hope you enjoy what you're about to read—my family's historical recipes, along with tips for making things turn out the best they can possibly be.

I have tweaked many recipes in this book to use modern ingredients, but all are snapshots of the way we Tennesseans cook, one dish at a time. I've also included a few memories of learning to cook, along with a little southern and soul food history.

As I said earlier, my culinary training came from the best—my family. But I did study business management at Dyersburg College in Dyersburg, Tennessee, and that education certainly has helped me as a food writer and in maintaining my popular website. I also enjoy talking and teaching about food, and over the years I've been a guest on radio programs, cooked on local television, and done cooking demos at restaurants, state fairs, and numerous festivals. Even more fun are book signings, where I can meet other home cooks face to face, and where we can share kitchen stories.

And why did I write this book? Because trends will come and go, but I'll always be a southern home cook at heart, and I want to pass on my family's legacy of authentic southern and soul cooking. I firmly believe that as long as we keep our stories real, keep the tradition alive, and make our recipes available to future generations, great cooking will never die.

CHAPTER 1

Why We Love One-Pot Meals

WHY are one-pot meals still popular in the South? The answer is simple—they're quick and easy to assemble, require little cleanup, and don't tie the cook down to the kitchen. Also, we southerners have a long history of cooking these dishes.

A one-pot meal is basically a combination of savory ingredients, such as meat, vegetables, beans, rice, pasta, or potatoes, and cooked together in a single vessel, whether it's in a skillet on top of the stove, in a Dutch oven, in a dish in an oven, or in a slow cooker. Every culture has its own versions, with recipes revolving around soups and stews, as well as the relatively new casserole. One-pot meals were common back when I was growing up in Halls, Tennessee, and they are still one of my favorites because they can usually be made ahead of time and leftovers are often enjoyed for several days. And most importantly, these hearty dishes are considered the "whole meal."

The tradition of cooking everything in the same pot goes back to Africa, where, for ages, dinner has often consisted of seasoned meats and/or a variety of vegetables cooked together in oil. This love of what is essentially a thick stew followed the Africans who were transported as slaves to the antebellum United States. Back then, working in fields 16 to 18 hours a day left little time and energy for cooking. Some plantations did provide communal meals. But for those who received meager, tough rations, a one-pot meal that could sit on an unattended fire all day was a virtual lifesaver.

For years after the Civil War, many rural southern cooks had to make do with whatever they found around the kitchen. And much too often that included inexpensive, chewy cuts of meat and foods that were almost spoiled. This lack of quality ingredients, coupled with the backbreaking work of running a home without modern appliances, made one-pot meals once again a necessity.

In today's South, even with a restaurant on every corner, a big pot of something home-cooked is as popular as ever. Many families are drawn together by the promise of cabbage and potatoes, macaroni and cheese, and collard greens with smoked turkey wings. Red beans and rice pop up at football parties, and spaghetti with meatballs and chicken and broccoli casserole often show up at funerals. And, no, most women don't work in fields like they did back in the day. But we still do appreciate the convenience of making delicious meals with minimal effort, and the bonus of not having to stay in the kitchen.

STEWED OKRA AND TOMATOES WITH SMOKED SAUSAGE

YIELD: 6—8 SERVINGS

Okra first came to the South in the 1660s through the African slave trade, and today it is an important ingredient in the popular New Orleans soup gumbo. As a matter of fact, many food historians believe the word "gumbo" comes from ngombo, the word for okra in the Bantu dialect of West Africa. Okra grows well all over the hot, humid South. In my childhood, my parents and I lived in the middle of the town of Halls, Tennessee, with my maternal grandmother, Big Mama, who grew okra in her summer garden and served the vegetable to us often.

2 tablespoons unsalted butter
⅔ cup chopped onion
1 pound sliced fresh or frozen okra (about 5 cups)
3 cups fresh chopped tomatoes, with any accumulated liquid
⅔ cup tomato juice or water
¼ teaspoon salt

¼ teaspoon ground black pepper
¼ teaspoon crushed red pepper
10–12 ounces smoked linked sausage, cut into 1-inch slices

1. In a large saucepan or Dutch oven, heat butter over medium
   heat. Add onion and cook, stirring frequently, until soft and
   translucent, about 3–5 minutes. Increase heat to high. Add
   okra, tomatoes, tomato juice, salt, black pepper, and crushed
   red pepper. Cook, stirring often, until mixture starts to bubble. Mix in sausage.
2. Reduce heat to a simmer and cook, stirring occasionally,
   until the mixture is thick and the vegetables are tender,
   about 20–30 minutes. Serve hot.

COUNTRY BLACK-EYED PEAS AND OKRA
YIELD: 6–8 SERVINGS

*The southern practice of eating black-eyed peas for good luck on New Year's Day
is believed to date back to the Civil War. Black-eyed peas came to America with
African slaves, and the undocumented legend is that when Major General Wil-
liam T. Sherman burned a large part of Georgia, he took everything edible except
stores of black-eyed peas, which were considered suitable only for animals. Sur-
vivors celebrated New Year's Day 1866 with the left-behind peas and felt lucky
they had that much to eat. Whether you choose to indulge in the southern New
Year's tradition or not, black-eyed peas are a good source of nutrition, low in fat,
contain no cholesterol, and are low in sodium.*

1 pound dried black-eyed peas, soaked overnight
   covered by 3 inches water
1 smoked turkey wing
⅔ cup chopped onion
Water
Seasoned salt to taste (purchased, or use recipe
   on pages 26–27)

Ground black pepper to taste

½ teaspoon ground red pepper (optional)

2 tablespoons white vinegar

2 cups chopped fresh or frozen okra

1. Rinse and drain soaked black-eyed peas and set aside. In a medium pot, add smoked turkey, onion, and enough water to cover turkey. Cover and cook over medium heat until turkey is just tender, about 2 hours.
2. Add peas, salt, black pepper, red pepper, and vinegar. Bring to a boil over high heat, reduce heat to low, and let black-eyed peas cook covered, until almost tender, about 45 minutes to 1 hour.
3. Add okra and continue cooking on low heat, covered. Stir occasionally and check for tenderness. Should be ready in about 30 more minutes, with juices thickened and peas and okra tender but not overcooked. Serve warm with skillet corn bread (recipe on pages 128–29).

COLLARD GREENS WITH SMOKED TURKEY

YIELD: ABOUT 6–8 SERVINGS

When my mother first taught me how to make collard greens, for years I served them to my family every Sunday. This was also the time I learned to perfect Big Mama's Hot-Water Corn Bread (recipe on pages 129–30). Nutritionists say collard greens are rich in calcium and loaded with vitamins A and C. I like to serve vitamin-packed collard greens over corn bread, which soaks up all that delicious potlikker, the leftover juice used to simmer the greens.

1 smoked turkey wing

4–6 cups water

1–2 hot pepper pods or 1 teaspoon crushed red
    pepper (optional)

1 cup chopped onion, divided

4 pounds fresh collard greens, divided
2 tablespoons white sugar
3 tablespoons vegetable or olive oil
3 tablespoons vinegar
Salt and pepper to taste

1. Place turkey wing in a large pot. Add water to cover, pepper pods, and ½ cup onion. Cover and bring to a boil. Reduce heat and simmer until meat is almost tender, about 2 hours.
2. Meanwhile, prepare greens for cooking (see below). To the meat pot, add half of prepared greens, sugar, oil, vinegar, remaining ½ cup onion, salt, and pepper.
3. Let the greens in the pot cook down for 15 minutes. Add the other half. Cover and cook over high heat until greens start to boil and have blended with the potlikker (juice). Reduce heat to medium. Cover and continue cooking for 45 minutes to 1 hour, or until greens are tender. Serve hot in a bowl with the potlikker, or use a slotted spoon to serve on a plate.

PREPARING COLLARD GREENS FOR COOKING
Wash greens:

1. Halfway fill a sink with cool water and add greens, being sure they are completely submerged.
2. Using both hands, dip a few leaves at a time in and out of the water. Remove cleaned leaves to a colander.
3. Repeat process for 2–3 washings, or until all dirt and grit is removed.

Prepare greens for cooking:

1. Starting from the pointed top of the greens, fold a leaf in half lengthwise and remove the large stem by tearing the leaf away from the stem and discarding stem.
2. Once the stems are removed, roll several leaves together like

a cigar and slice the rolls into bite-sized pieces, in about ¼-inch strips.

3. Repeat the process until all greens have been cut into bite-sized pieces.

TIP: If you purchase fresh greens from the grocery store, make sure that they are healthy-looking and the leaves have not yellowed. Fresh or frozen greens already prepared and packaged in plastic bags typically have the stems cut up with the greens, so when you cook them you will be cooking the stems along with the greens. This will not give you a true collard greens experience. It's best to select fresh greens that are not from a plastic bag.

SEASONED CABBAGE WITH WHITE POTATOES
YIELD: 4–6 SERVINGS

Cabbage is one of my favorite vegetables, and it's incredibly nutritious. One cup of leaves provides just 25 calories, and it's a good source of vitamins A and K and helps reduce LDL ("bad cholesterol") levels in the blood. This is another recipe that is good served with skillet corn bread (recipe on pages 128–29), and the combo is truly a southern favorite.

3 ounces salt pork or smoked ham, diced into ¼-inch pieces, or
    4 slices bacon, cut in half
4 cups water
6 cups cabbage, cut into bite-sized pieces
⅔ cup chopped onion
2 tablespoons vegetable oil
Seasoned salt, to taste (purchased, or use recipe on pages 26–27)
Ground black pepper, to taste
½ teaspoon red pepper (optional)
2 tablespoons vinegar
2 cups peeled and quartered white potatoes, or substitute
    red potatoes

1. In a medium covered pot, boil pork with water over medium heat until just tender, 10–15 minutes.
2. Add cabbage, onion, oil, seasoned salt, black pepper, red pepper, and vinegar. Cover and cook over medium-low heat until cabbage is just tender, about 15 minutes.
3. Add potatoes and cook until both cabbage and potatoes are fork-tender, about 15 more minutes. Serve hot.

MAMIE'S TURKEY POT PIE
YIELD: 3–4 SERVINGS

I remember eating a lot of turkey pot pies as a young girl. This is a really old recipe that comes from the recipe collection of my mother, Mamie, and she created it in the 1960s. And not only is this flaky pot pie mouthwateringly savory and satisfying, but it's inexpensive to put together.

2 (9-inch) pie crusts (recipe follows)
4 tablespoons unsalted butter, divided
⅔ cup minced onion
2 stalks celery, chopped
2 carrots, diced
2 tablespoons chopped fresh parsley
1 tablespoon fresh oregano
1 teaspoon seasoned salt (purchased, or use
  recipe on pages 26–27)
1 teaspoon ground black pepper
2 cups water
2 cups red or white peeled and cubed potatoes
1½ cups chopped cooked turkey
3 tablespoons all-purpose flour
½ cup whole milk

1. Preheat oven to 425°F. Place one pie crust in an ungreased 9-inch pie dish. Set aside.

2. In a large skillet, heat 2 tablespoons butter over medium heat and sauté onion, celery, carrots, parsley, oregano, salt, and pepper. Cook and stir until vegetables are tender. Stir in the water. Bring to a boil. Stir in the potatoes and cook until tender but still firm. Set aside.

3. In a medium saucepan, melt the remaining 2 tablespoons butter over low heat and stir in the turkey and flour. Add milk and heat until small bubbles appear. Add the turkey mixture to the vegetable mixture. Cook over medium heat until mixture thickens.

4. Pour mixture into the pie crust. Top with the other pie crust and seal edges by crimping with a damp fork. Vent pie crust by cutting 2–4 slits on the top crust. Bake 15 minutes. Reduce oven temperature to 350°F and continue baking until crust is golden brown, about 20 more minutes. Allow to sit at least 10 minutes before serving.

FLAKY PIE CRUST

YIELD: TWO 9-INCH PIE CRUSTS

2½ cups all-purpose flour
1 teaspoon salt
1 cup solid vegetable shortening (preferably nonhydrogenated)
¼ cup ice water, plus 1 teaspoon (or more, as needed)

1. In a medium bowl, sift together flour and salt. Cut in the shortening until mixture is the texture of coarse crumbs. Add water and mix with a fork until dough starts to come together. Form dough into 2 balls and flatten each.

2. Wrap the dough pieces in wax paper or plastic wrap and store in the refrigerator 30 minutes. When ready to roll dough, do so on a cool and dry floured surface. For a 9-inch pan, roll into 11-inch circles.

CREAMY CHICKEN, BROCCOLI, AND RICE CASSEROLE

YIELD: 6–8 SERVINGS

Cooking in covered clay pots has been around since prehistoric times, but America didn't embrace the modern casserole until the late nineteenth century, when it became a good way to stretch a food dollar during the 1890s depression. Since then, casseroles sure have become a staple of southern cooking and can still make a delicious and inexpensive meal.

½ cup (8 tablespoons) unsalted butter, divided
⅓ cup finely chopped onion
⅓ cup finely chopped green pepper
1 cup chopped fresh mushrooms
2 tablespoons all-purpose flour
1 cup half-and-half
1 cup whole milk
2 cups shredded Cheddar cheese, divided
1½ cups chicken broth or stock (purchased, or use recipe
    on pages 65–66)
2 cups fresh broccoli, cut into small pieces and steamed until
    half-done
1 cup cooked and deboned chicken
2 cups cooked rice
1 teaspoon seasoned salt (purchased, or use recipe
    on pages 26–27)
½ teaspoon ground black pepper
½ teaspoon dried thyme
1 tablespoon chopped, fresh parsley

1. Preheat oven to 350°F. In a large skillet over medium-high heat, melt 4 tablespoons butter and sauté onion and green pepper until onion is translucent, about 3–5 minutes. Set aside.
2. In a medium pan, melt remaining 4 tablespoons butter and cook mushrooms until they release their liquid. Whisk in the flour and cook until smooth. Add sautéed vegetables to mushroom mixture. Mix well.

3. Add half-and-half, whole milk, 1½ cups of cheese, and broth. Cook over low heat until cheese is melted, stirring constantly. Add broccoli, chicken, rice, and seasoned salt. Mix well and check for seasoning.

4. Pour into a 9×13–inch buttered casserole dish. Sprinkle remaining ½ cup of cheese on top, and sprinkle thyme and parsley on top of cheese. Bake casserole until thick and bubbles appear around the edges, about 25–30 minutes. Serve hot.

TIP: You can also freeze the unbaked casserole in a dish and bake later.

TENNESSEE–STYLE CHICKEN WINGS WITH VEGETABLES

YIELD: 6–8 SERVINGS

1½ pounds chicken wings
⅓ cup vegetable oil
⅔ cup chopped green pepper
⅔ cup chopped onion
1 pound ground beef
1 (14.5-ounce) can chopped tomatoes, with liquid
1 cup chicken broth or stock (purchased, or use recipe on pages 65–66)
1 teaspoon fresh thyme
½ teaspoon ground allspice
⅛ teaspoon cayenne pepper (optional)
⅛ teaspoon ground black pepper
⅛ teaspoon seasoned salt (purchased, or use recipe on pages 26–27)
⅔ cup cooked lima beans, drained
⅔ cup cooked corn kernels, drained
8 slices cooked bacon, crumbled
Hot cooked rice for serving

1. Remove and discard chicken wing tips, and reserve remain-

ing wings. Heat oil in large skillet over medium heat and fry wings until slightly brown. Transfer wings to a platter.

2. To same skillet, add green pepper and onion, and sauté until crisp-tender. Stir in beef and cook until done. Drain off fat and transfer to a large pot.

3. To pot, add browned wings, tomatoes, broth, thyme, allspice, cayenne pepper, black pepper, and seasoned salt. Cover and cook until wings are tender, about 15–20 minutes. Add lima beans and corn and simmer until vegetables are hot, about 5–10 minutes.

4. Transfer to a serving bowl and top with bacon. Serve over hot cooked rice.

CHICKEN AND FROM-SCRATCH DUMPLINGS

YIELD: ABOUT 6–8 SERVINGS

Chicken and dumplings is a popular dish in the southern and midwestern United States. And it's another one of those down-home dinner classics that's prepared with variations depending on your region. Wherever you live, chicken and dumplings is a satisfying, inexpensive meal perfectly suited for family dining in the fall and winter.

3 pounds skinless, boneless chicken breasts
Water
1 cup chopped onion
2 carrots, chopped
3 stalks celery, chopped
4 cloves garlic, finely chopped
2 dried bay leaves
1 tablespoon fresh chopped thyme
2 tablespoons fresh chopped parsley, divided
2 teaspoons salt, divided
½ teaspoon ground black pepper
1 teaspoon dried coriander

½ teaspoon cayenne pepper

1 cup all-purpose flour

2 teaspoons baking powder

½ cup whole milk

1. Place chicken in a large pot with enough water to cover chicken. Add onion, carrots, celery, garlic, bay leaves, thyme, 1 tablespoon parsley, 1½ teaspoons salt, black pepper, coriander, and cayenne pepper. Cover and bring to a boil over medium-high heat. Reduce to low heat and simmer until chicken is tender, about 35–45 minutes.

2. Remove chicken from broth and wait until cool enough to handle. Cut chicken into large chunks and set aside. Remove bay leaves from broth and discard. Skim as much fat as possible from the surface of the broth. Heat broth to a boil.

3. Make dumplings: In a medium bowl, combine flour, baking powder, and remaining ½ teaspoon salt. Stir in milk and mix to make a stiff batter. Drop tablespoons of batter, 1 at a time, into the boiling broth. Cover and cook 10 minutes.

4. Add reserved chicken and cook until heated through, about 5 minutes. The dumplings should be puffed and the meat warmed throughout. Garnish with remaining parsley and serve immediately in bowls.

CHICKEN AND CORN BREAD DRESSING WITH GIBLET GRAVY

YIELD: 10–12 SERVINGS

This is the way my mom made chicken and dressing, with a whole chicken sitting on top of the dressing, and everything cooked in one dish. And, of course, her recipe is the one I still use for corn bread dressing.

I have discovered that by baking the onions, peppers, and celery in the corn bread batter, the seasoning vegetable flavors are more intense throughout the dressing. For an extra-special treat, slice off part of the baked, crusted edges of the corn bread, hot from the oven, and enjoy them slathered with butter. (My husband actually gets upset if I don't butter him some of those crispy crusts.) Without question, this recipe is always the shining star on my holiday dining table.

1 whole roasting chicken or hen, with giblets
Water
2 cups finely chopped white onion, divided
2 cups finely chopped celery, divided
2 cups finely chopped green pepper, divided
3 tablespoons poultry seasoning, divided
2 tablespoons salt, divided
2 tablespoons black pepper, divided
2 tablespoons rubbed sage, divided
⅓ cup vegetable oil
2 cups self-rising cornmeal
2 tablespoons all-purpose flour
1½ cups whole milk
2 large eggs, slightly beaten
4 cups homemade broth (see below), more if needed, divided
4 slices stale white bread, torn into small chunks
4 hard-boiled eggs, chopped
Ground paprika
Giblet Gravy (recipe follows)

1. Remove giblets from inside chicken and rinse chicken in clear water. In a large pot, add chicken and giblets with enough water to just cover chicken. Add 1 cup onion, 1 cup celery, and 1 cup green pepper to pot. Add 1 tablespoon poultry seasoning, 1 tablespoon salt, 1 tablespoon black pepper, and 1 tablespoon sage. Cover and cook on high heat until chicken starts to boil. Reduce heat and continue cooking until just tender, about 45 minutes to 1 hour.
2. Remove chicken and giblets from pot and set aside. Let whole chicken cool. Reserve giblets for gravy. *Important:* Do not discard liquid; this is your homemade broth, so set it aside, too.
3. Make corn bread for dressing: Preheat oven to 375°F. In

oven, heat oil in a 10-inch cast-iron skillet or a 2-quart baking pan until oil is hot but not smoking hot. While oil is heating, in a large bowl, mix the cornmeal, flour, milk, eggs, remaining onion, celery, and green pepper. Mix well. Pour mixture in hot oil and bake until the top is golden brown, 20–30 minutes.

4. Remove cooked corn bread from the skillet and put it in a 9 × 13–inch roasting pan. Cool slightly and break into bite-sized pieces. Add remaining 2 tablespoons poultry seasoning, 1 tablespoon salt (or to taste), remaining 1 tablespoon black pepper, and remaining 1 tablespoon sage. Mix well. Add 2 cups broth, torn white bread, and chopped eggs. Mix well and add more salt and pepper if needed. *Very important:* Mixture should not be soupy or dry. Add more broth or torn bread as needed. Spread dressing evenly in roasting pan and place the whole cooked chicken in the center on top of the dressing.

5. Sprinkle paprika over chicken. Bake, uncovered, until chicken is heated through and dressing starts to form a light-brown crust around the edges, about 40–50 minutes. Serve hot.

TIP: It's best to make the dressing 1–2 days before serving, then wrap tightly, unbaked, and store in the refrigerator. This allows the spices to mingle and develop, making the dressing more flavorful. If made ahead, add more broth or water before baking. This dressing holds up well in the refrigerator, covered, for 3–5 days. It also freezes well.

GIBLET GRAVY

YIELD: ABOUT 2½ CUPS

4 tablespoons vegetable oil
¼ cup finely chopped onion
2 tablespoons all-purpose flour

2 cups chicken broth or water
½ cup whole milk or half-and-half
1 teaspoon seasoned salt (purchased, or use
   recipe on pages 26–27)
½ teaspoon black pepper, or to taste
2 hard-boiled eggs, chopped
Cooked giblets from 1 roasting chicken, chopped

1. In a small skillet over medium heat, heat oil until hot. Add
   onion and sauté until translucent, about 3–5 minutes.
2. Add flour and stir until light brown, about 3 minutes. Stir
   in broth and add milk, salt, and black pepper. Mix well.
3. Add eggs and giblets. Reduce heat and simmer until gravy
   thickens. Serve over dressing.

TENNESSEE-STYLE RED BEANS AND RICE WITH SMOKED SAUSAGE

YIELD: 6–8 SERVINGS

Of course we eat red beans in Tennessee! This popular southern dish originated in New Orleans with the Spanish. In that city it was traditional for housewives to keep a big pot of red beans simmering while they did the laundry on Monday. Today, still, red beans and rice is the traditional Monday dish in New Orleans. This version is made with tomatoes, the way we like to make it in Tennessee.

1 cup uncooked white rice
2 cups water
2 tablespoons bacon fat
⅔ cup chopped onion
⅔ cup chopped green pepper
2 tablespoons minced garlic
2 stalks celery, chopped
⅛ cup chopped shallots
1 teaspoon red pepper
Seasoned salt to taste (purchased, or use recipe
   on pages 26–27)

Ground black pepper to taste

16 ounces cooked, smoked linked sausage, cut into 1-inch slices

1 (15-ounce) can kidney beans, drained

1 (14.5-ounce) can diced tomatoes, with liquid

½ cup water

1. In a medium pot, bring rice and water to a boil. Cover, reduce heat to low and simmer until tender, about 15 minutes. Set aside, covered.
2. In a large skillet over medium heat, add bacon fat, onion, green pepper, garlic, celery, and shallots. Cook until tender. Add red pepper, seasoned salt, and black pepper.
3. Stir in sausage and cook until slightly brown. Add rice to sausage mixture and mix well. Add beans, tomatoes, and water. Blend well and continue cooking until heated through thoroughly. Serve warm.

MACARONI, CHEESE, AND SAUSAGE CASSEROLE

YIELD: 6–8 SERVINGS

Some believe that President Thomas Jefferson, a great lover of cheese and Italian food, brought a macaroni-making machine back from Italy and that he served macaroni and cheese at White House dinner parties. Today, macaroni and cheese is considered the most popular American comfort food, and it is a staple dish in many homes in the South, especially in those with children.

12 ounces uncooked elbow macaroni

2 tablespoons unsalted butter, softened

1 teaspoon yellow prepared mustard

16 ounces shredded Cheddar cheese, divided

Seasoned salt to taste (purchased, or use recipe on pages 26–27)

Ground black pepper to taste

1–1½ cups whole milk

½ cup sour cream

1 large egg

10–12 ounces smoked, cooked, linked sausages, cut
    into 1-inch slices

1 tablespoon chopped fresh parsley

1. Preheat oven to 350°F. Cook macaroni according to package
   directions. Drain. In a large bowl, combine cooked macaroni,
   butter, mustard, half the cheese, seasoned salt, black pepper,
   whole milk, sour cream, and egg. Add sausage; mix well.
2. Transfer to a 9×13–inch buttered casserole dish.
3. Sprinkle the top with remaining cheese and parsley. Cover
   and bake 20–25 minutes. Serve warm.

BEEF AND TOMATO CASSEROLE

YIELD: 4–6 SERVINGS

½ pound ground beef

⅔ cup chopped celery

⅔ cup chopped onion

⅔ cup chopped green pepper

2 teaspoons Worcestershire sauce

1 teaspoon salt

½ teaspoon chopped fresh basil

¼ teaspoon black pepper

2 cups uncooked (medium) egg noodles

1 (16-ounce) can kidney beans, rinsed and drained

1 (14.5-ounce) can stewed tomatoes, with liquid

1 cup water

1. In a large saucepan or skillet, cook ground beef over medium-high heat until no longer pink; drain.
2. Add celery, onion, and green pepper; cook 5 minutes or
   until vegetables are crisp-tender. Add Worcestershire sauce,

salt, basil, and black pepper.

3. Stir in noodles, beans, tomatoes, and water. Bring to a boil. Reduce heat; cover and simmer 20–25 minutes, or until noodles are tender; stirring occasionally. Serve hot.

SOUTHERN–STYLE SPAGHETTI WITH GROUND BEEF
YIELD: 8–10 SERVINGS

In my family, instead of making meatballs to go alongside spaghetti, we put crumbled ground beef in the sauce. We like our spaghetti smothered in thick tomato sauce and melted cheese, and we expect to have meat in every bite. This recipe is similar to Memphis-style spaghetti, which is made with ground beef instead of traditional meatballs and with the meat, pasta, and tomato sauce all mixed together, instead of the sauce served on the side. This old family favorite is, to us, best served with catfish, coleslaw, and skillet corn bread. This combo may sound odd to you, but if these four dishes aren't served together, we feel something is missing.

1 (7-ounce) package uncooked spaghetti
1 teaspoon garlic salt
3 tablespoons vegetable oil
⅔ cup chopped onion
⅔ cup chopped green pepper
1 pound ground beef (chuck or round)
2 teaspoons minced fresh garlic
1 (6-ounce) can tomato paste
1 cup water
1 (8-ounce) can tomato sauce
½ cup ketchup
1 teaspoon chopped fresh oregano
2 teaspoons chopped fresh basil
1 (14-ounce) can chopped stewed tomatoes, with liquid
Seasoned salt to taste (purchased, or use recipe
    on pages 26–27)

Ground black pepper to taste
3 dashes red hot sauce (optional)
1 cup grated Cheddar cheese, divided
Chopped, fresh parsley

1. In a large pot, cook spaghetti according to package directions. Drain and season with garlic salt. Set aside.
2. In a large skillet, heat vegetable oil over medium-high heat and sauté onion and green pepper until onion is translucent, about 3–5 minutes. Add ground beef and cook until no longer pink.
3. Drain oil and add minced garlic, tomato paste, water, tomato sauce, ketchup, oregano, and basil. Mix well and cook over low heat until well blended and mixture just starts to simmer.
4. Add beef mixture to cooked spaghetti. Stir in tomatoes, salt, black pepper, and hot sauce. Mix well. Add more water if necessary. Sprinkle ½ cup cheese into spaghetti mixture and mix well. Sprinkle remaining cheese and parsley over spaghetti. Cover and simmer until cheese starts to melt. Serve hot.

TIP: This recipe can also be topped with the remaining cheese and parsley then baked in the oven at 350°F in a 9 × 13–inch buttered casserole dish for 25–35 minutes.

VEGETABLE, SCALLOP, AND SHRIMP STEW
YIELD: 4–6 SERVINGS

My family loves seafood, so back in the 1980s I reworked an old recipe I had in my collection and came up with this nutritious dish.

2 teaspoons olive oil
⅔ cup minced onion
½ teaspoon dried thyme

½ teaspoon dried fennel seed

¼ teaspoon salt

¼ teaspoon ground black pepper

1 clove garlic, minced

1 cup diced tomatoes, with liquid

¼ cup vegetable stock (purchased, or use recipe
  on pages 67–68)

4 ounces fresh green beans, cooked

4 ounces fresh yellow corn, steamed until almost done

4 ounces bay scallops (defrosted if frozen)

6 ounces small shrimp (defrosted if frozen)

1. In a large saucepan or skillet, heat oil over medium heat.
   Add onion and cook, stirring constantly, for 3 minutes. Add
   thyme, fennel seed, salt, and black pepper. Cook a few more
   minutes.
2. Stir in minced garlic, tomatoes, vegetable stock, green
   beans, and corn. Cover and bring to a simmer. Cook until
   slightly thickened, about 5–7 minutes.
3. Increase heat to medium-high. Stir in scallops and cook,
   stirring occasionally, for 2 minutes. Add shrimp and cook,
   stirring occasionally, until shrimp are cooked through,
   about 3 minutes. Serve hot in soup bowls.

SEAFOOD STEW

YIELD: 6–8 SERVINGS

*This stew is so flavorful and jam-packed with seafood that once you make it,
you'll find yourself serving it often. My family craves this dish, especially during
the cooler months. If you love seafood like I do, then this is your dish.*

¼ cup vegetable oil

½ cup chopped onion

1 teaspoon garlic salt

2 tablespoons all-purpose flour

2 teaspoons minced garlic

4 cups seafood or vegetable stock (purchased, or use
    recipes on pages 66–68)

3 (14.5-ounce) cans of coarsely chopped stewed tomatoes, with
    liquid

½ teaspoon red pepper flakes (optional)

3 large dashes red hot sauce

1 teaspoon seasoned salt (purchased, or use recipe just below)

1 teaspoon ground black pepper

12 ounces Polish or your favorite cooked, linked sausage, cut
    into 1-inch slices

12 ounces coarsely chopped crabmeat

12 ounces medium cooked, peeled shrimp

Cooked hot rice for serving.

1. In a large pot over medium heat, add oil and sauté onion
   until translucent, about 3–5 minutes. Season with garlic salt.
   Add flour and cook until lightly browned, 3–5 minutes.
2. Remove from heat. Add minced garlic and mix well. Return
   to heat.
3. Add stock, tomatoes, red pepper flakes, red hot sauce, seasoned salt, and black pepper. Stir and let cook until mixture
   starts to boil. Reduce heat to medium.
4. Add sausage, crabmeat, and shrimp, and cook until thoroughly heated, about 5–10 minutes. Serve over rice.

CASSANDRA'S SEASONED SALT
YIELD: ABOUT 1 CUP

*This is my recipe for seasoned salt. It's best with beef, pork, vegetables, soups,
and stews, but I use this blend whenever possible because it gives my cooking its
signature flavor, making my dishes stand out from the rest. This recipe is inexpensive to make and will keep at room temperature up to a year in an airtight
container.*

⅔ cup fine sea salt

1 teaspoon white sugar (optional)

5 tablespoons paprika

1 tablespoon onion powder

1 tablespoon garlic powder

1 teaspoon ground black pepper

1 teaspoon ground turmeric

¼ teaspoon dried marjoram

¼ teaspoon dried thyme

Combine everything in a small bowl. Store in an airtight container for up to 1 year.

CHAPTER 2

Heritage Entrées

HERE are a few main dishes that can serve as the foundation for any great southern meal. They're not what you'd call fancy or trendy. But they are good, basic entrées that don't require much fuss, and they're cooked the way we do it in southwest Tennessee. My family always loved cooking together, as many southern families still do today, and before we thought about sides, we first decided on an entrée. Even with today's fast pace, I still take time to prepare a great meal that's built around beef, poultry, pork, or fish.

I suppose you can define a heritage entrée as one that will never go out of style, one that people will never tire of. In fact, we look forward to these familiar dishes not just for their taste but for the memories of dining on them in the past.

Although Big Mama excelled at cooking just about everything, one of my most precious memories of my grandmother revolves around her pressing a meat loaf into a baking pan. And I'll never forget the scent of her sweet and salty baked ham slices. Also, it was so, so comforting to hear the sizzle of chicken frying in the skillet; aside from gardening, not much else brought more joy to Big Mama than gathering the family and serving her crispy fried chicken.

Too, I remember Sundays, when the preacher came for dinner, and my mom would make her tender pot roast drowned in brown onion gravy. She would also whip up her famous homemade mashed potatoes (sure wish I'd gotten that recipe), and she would cook whatever fresh vegetables she could find in Big Mama's garden. Oh, what a delicious meal that was. I still make my pot roast the way my mom made hers—that's the only way I know.

My dad, Emerson, was the fisherman in the family. On Saturday mornings he'd go to a nearby lake where he typically caught enough catfish for several meals. I remember one time he caught so many fish that I thought there were no more fish left in that lake. The neighbors loved for him to go on those fishing trips, too, because he was always happy to share his catch.

Aside from bringing fish home, my dad was the designated fish-fryer, and for a big family meal he would fry up several skillets. We'd eat the day's catch with sides of coleslaw, and we'd pour red hot sauce all over the hot fish. Mmmm, it makes me hungry just thinking about it.

The memories of Big Mama's meat loaf and my dad's catfish are still with me when I plan family menus. And we do dine as a family often. You may think this sounds old-fashioned, but I believe that enjoying great food with everyone around the table is still the glue that keeps families together. And unless you're a vegetarian, these meals that bind need a protein-packed and filling focal point—yes, they need meat as an anchor.

COUNTRY SMOTHERED HAM
YIELD: 2–3 SERVINGS

Moist, slightly sweet, and full of savory flavor, this recipe is a spectacular entrée at dinner and for special breakfasts.

    2 slices country ham, cut ½-inch thick (uncooked)
    2 teaspoons dry mustard, divided
    2 cups pared, sliced apples
    1 cup chopped onions
    10 whole cloves
    1 cup light brown sugar

½ cup water

1 teaspoon ground cinnamon

1. Preheat oven to 350°F. Place 1 slice of ham in a 9 × 13–inch baking pan; spread 1 teaspoon of mustard on ham. Top with apples and onions; cover with second slice of ham. Rub remaining mustard onto meat. Stick cloves in fat portion of ham.

2. In a saucepan, mix together brown sugar, water, and cinnamon. Boil over medium heat until syrupy, about 5 minutes. Pour ⅔ cup syrup mixture over ham.

3. Bake for 1 hour. As ham bakes baste with remaining syrup mixture. Serve ham warm.

BIG MAMA'S OLD-FASHIONED MEAT LOAF

YIELD: ABOUT 10–12 SERVINGS

One of my great memories of family dinners was when Big Mama made her old-fashioned meat loaf. This delicious recipe is light on the budget yet jam-packed full of flavor, and it is a great centerpiece dish for a family dinner.

2 pounds ground beef (or 1 pound ground beef and
    1 pound ground pork loin)

1 cup seasoned bread crumbs

2 eggs, beaten

⅓ cup finely chopped onions

⅓ cup finely chopped green bell peppers

2 dashes Worcestershire Sauce

2 teaspoons salt

¼ teaspoon ground black pepper

¼ teaspoon dry mustard

⅛ teaspoon garlic salt

⅛ teaspoon celery salt

½ cup cold water

MEAT LOAF SAUCE

½ cup ketchup
¼ cup brown sugar
1 teaspoon brown mustard
Dried parsley flakes

1. Preheat oven to 350°F. In a large mixing bowl, combine the ground beef and ground pork. Add the bread crumbs, eggs, onions, bell peppers, Worcestershire sauce, salt, pepper, mustard, garlic salt, celery salt, and water. Mix well.
2. Pack meat loaf into a buttered 9½ × 4½–inch loaf pan.
3. Make sauce: In a small bowl, mix together ketchup, brown sugar, and brown mustard. Spread ketchup mixture on top of meat loaf. Sprinkle parsley flakes on top. Bake until well-done, about 1½ hours. Allow to cool 15 minutes at room temperature. Slice into serving pieces and serve hot.

CHICKEN-FRIED STEAK WITH CREAMY GRAVY

YIELD: ABOUT 6–8 SERVINGS

Food historians say that chicken-fried steak (a pounded beef steak fried similar to fried chicken) has been a staple dish of the South, Southwest, and Midwest for decades. It is also believed that chicken-fried steak began showing up in American print in the 1920s, and that in the 1930s, this dish was a popular yet inexpensive dish favored by Depression-era cooks. Many believe that dredging any type of meat in flour and spices, frying or baking it up, and serving it with a sauce or gravy dates back to ancient times. Regardless, this cooking method tenderizes a tough cut of meat and enhances its flavor. This is a wonderful country recipe the entire family will enjoy.

6–8 portions beef cube steak (3–3½ pounds, pounded and tenderized to about ¼ inch thick)

Seasoned salt to taste (purchased, or use recipe
   on pages 26–27)
Ground black pepper
2 cups whole milk
2 large eggs
3 cups all-purpose flour
1 teaspoon cayenne pepper
1 teaspoon garlic salt
1 teaspoon finely chopped fresh parsley
Vegetable oil for frying
Creamy Gravy (recipe follows)

1. Spread the steaks on a sheet pan. Season meat well with seasoned salt and ground black pepper on each side. Set aside.
2. Set out 2 shallow bowls and a plate in a row. In the first dish on the left, mix together the milk and eggs. In the middle dish, put in flour, cayenne, garlic salt, and parsley. Mix well. The plate is for holding the breaded meat before it's fried.
3. Dip a seasoned steak in milk/egg mixture. Next, place the meat into the seasoned flour and coat well on all sides. Then place meat back into the milk/egg mixture and back into the seasoned flour. Shake off excess flour; place steak on the clean plate.
4. Repeat process for the remaining steaks.
5. Heat ½ inch vegetable oil until hot in a large cast-iron skillet over medium heat. Place a few pieces of breaded meat in skillet but do not overcrowd. Cook meat until edges start to get golden brown; around 3–5 minutes per side.
6. Place steak on a paper towel and keep warm. Repeat frying process with remaining steak. Serve warm topped with Creamy Gravy.

CREAMY GRAVY

YIELD: ABOUT 2 CUPS

¼ cup grease from steak pan
⅓ cup all-purpose flour
¼ cup finely chopped green bell peppers
¼ cup finely chopped onions
1½–2 cups whole milk (more if needed), divided
Seasoned salt to taste (purchased, or use recipe
   on pages 26–27)
Ground black pepper to taste
Dash of red hot sauce (optional)

1. Heat grease over medium heat in the same pan used to fry steaks. Slowly add the flour, green peppers, and onions and whisk until flour turns golden brown, 3–5 minutes.
2. Continue whisking and slowly add 1 cup of milk. As the mixture cooks it will start to thicken. If mixture thickens too much, add more milk, about ¼ cup at a time. Continue to whisk.
3. Add seasoned salt, black pepper, and red hot sauce. Reduce heat to low and cook, whisking constantly, until gravy is thick and very smooth, 5–10 minutes. Taste to make sure gravy is seasoned properly. Serve gravy hot over chicken-fried steak.

MAMA'S SUNDAY POT ROAST WITH BROWN ONION GRAVY

YIELD: ABOUT 8 SERVINGS

My mom mostly made this dish on Sundays after church services, when we all gathered around the table as the pastor came over for dinner. The smell of her juicy roast smothered in brown onion gravy with fresh garden vegetables brings back so many great memories. This old-time favorite is extremely popular throughout the South, and I don't think it will ever go out of style.

1 boneless beef chuck roast (4–5 pounds), fat
    trimmed and tied
2 teaspoons garlic powder
½ teaspoon seasoned salt (purchased, or use recipe
    on pages 26–27)
½ teaspoon ground black pepper
½ teaspoon fresh thyme
All-purpose flour
⅓ cup vegetable oil
Water
⅔ cup chopped onion
⅔ cup chopped green pepper
2 celery stalks, sliced
4 thin carrots, scraped and sliced
2 cups red or white peeled and quartered potatoes
1 tablespoon chopped fresh parsley
Brown Onion Gravy (recipe follows)

1. Preheat oven to 350°F. Rinse roast and pat dry. Season with garlic powder, seasoned salt, black pepper, and thyme. Coat with flour on all sides.
2. In a large skillet, heat oil over medium-high heat and brown roast evenly until a crust forms. Place roast in a large baking pan with enough water to cover halfway up the roast. Add onion, green pepper, and celery. Cover and bake until roast starts to get tender, about 2 hours.
3. Add carrots and potatoes and sprinkle with parsley. Continue baking until meat and vegetables are fork-tender, about 45 more minutes.
4. Remove meat to a warm platter and cover. Strain drippings and use liquid to make Brown Onion Gravy. Serve warm roast with gravy.

BROWN ONION GRAVY

YIELD: 2 CUPS

4 tablespoons vegetable oil
¼ cup chopped onion
¼ cup chopped green pepper
2 tablespoons all-purpose flour
2 cups beef drippings, beef stock, or water
½ teaspoon seasoned salt (purchased, or use
   recipe on pages 26–27)
½ teaspoon ground black pepper

1. In a small skillet over medium heat, heat oil until hot. Add onion and green pepper and sauté until vegetables are translucent, 3–5 minutes.
2. Add flour and stir until light brown, about 3 minutes.
3. Add drippings, seasoned salt, and black pepper. Stir until mixture begins to boil. Simmer until gravy thickens. Serve over pot roast.

SOUTHERN FRIED CHICKEN

YIELD: 4–6 SERVINGS

My first experience with fried chicken was when I was about ten years old. One day my mom was late coming home from work, and my older sister, Debra, and I were getting hungry so we decided to take a whole fryer from the refrigerator and cut it up. Back then, you couldn't purchase chicken parts like you can today, and I had never cut up a chicken before. But between the two of us, we managed to hack that chicken into pieces. We had watched our mom fry chicken several times so we followed her technique. We rinsed the chicken off, seasoned it, then smothered it with flour. After the oil got hot, we were ready to fry. When mom got home, she was not happy that we had cut the chicken up and fried it by ourselves. But she soon got over that and had to admit that we did a pretty good job with our first fried chicken.

3½ pounds chicken, cut up or chicken parts
Seasoned salt to taste (purchased, or use
    recipe on pages 26–27)
Ground black pepper
1½–2 cups all-purpose flour
2 teaspoons garlic salt
1 teaspoon paprika
Vegetable oil for frying

1. Rinse chicken off in clear water and pat some of the moisture off. Lightly season chicken with seasoned salt and black pepper; set aside.
2. In a paper or plastic bag, combine flour, garlic salt, paprika, and seasoned salt and black pepper to taste. Mix well.
3. Dip chicken into flour and coat well on all sides. Shake off excess flour.
4. Heat 2 inches oil to 350°F in a cast-iron skillet over medium heat. Fry 4 pieces of chicken until deep golden brown and the juices inside run clear, about 10–20 minutes, depending on the chicken part. Keep skillet uncovered and turn the pieces often. Drain on paper towels. Repeat process until all pieces are fried. Serve warm or cold.

FRIED CATFISH FILLETS

YIELD: 4–5 SERVINGS

My dad used to go fishing a lot, and he would catch crappies and catfish. Although we southerners think the catfish is ours alone, catfish are most diverse in tropical South America, Asia, and Africa, with only one family native to Europe, and one to North America. Catfish used to be considered the food of the poor, but more and more chefs are beginning to create new ways to serve this earthy-tasting fish. Most small-town restaurants in the South feature catfish on their menus, and, believe it or not, catfish is the most widely eaten fish in America. There are many ways to prepare catfish, but most southerners prefer it dredged in cornmeal and fried. Catfish is my favorite fish to cook, and I, too, like mine fried and served with Southern-Style Coleslaw (recipe on pages 74–75).

Vegetable oil for deep frying
8–10 catfish or perch fillets
4 tablespoons seasoned salt (purchased, or use recipe on pages 26–27), divided
2 teaspoons ground black pepper
½ teaspoon paprika
¾ teaspoon onion powder
3 tablespoons all-purpose flour
1¼ cups cornmeal (more if needed)

1. Heat 2 inches vegetable oil in a deep-fryer or skillet to 375°F. (I prefer using my cast-iron skillet.)
2. Wash fish and pat dry. Lightly season with 2 tablespoons seasoned salt and set aside.
3. In a medium bowl, combine remaining 2 tablespoons seasoned salt, black pepper, paprika, and onion powder. Mix. Add flour and cornmeal to spices. Mix well.
4. Coat fillets in cornmeal mixture. Let set about 10 minutes then coat again. Shake off excess cornmeal.
5. Deep-fry fish until golden-brown on each side. Drain on paper towels and serve immediately. (I like eating mine with red hot sauce.)

OVEN-FRIED PORK CHOPS
YIELD: 6 SERVINGS

We were always taught to cook pork thoroughly, but a few years ago, the USDA lowered the safe temperature for cooking pork from 160°F to 145°F, with a 3-minute resting time. If you don't like dry pork, then this revised guideline is good news for you!

3 tablespoons unsalted butter, melted

2 eggs, well beaten

⅓ cup whole milk

2 teaspoons seasoned salt (purchased, or use recipe on pages 26–27)

1 teaspoon ground black pepper

½ teaspoon garlic powder

½ teaspoon paprika

6 (1-inch thick) pork chops, bone in and trimmed

1½ cups herb-seasoned stuffing mix

1. Preheat oven to 375°F. Pour melted butter into a 9 × 13–inch baking pan. Set aside.
2. In a medium bowl, mix together eggs, milk, seasoned salt, black pepper, garlic powder, and paprika. Mix well.
3. Dip pork chops in egg mixture; coat each chop well with stuffing mix; place in prepared baking pan.
4. Bake 10 minutes. Turn chops and bake another 10–15 minutes, or until the pink areas have just disappeared and the juices run clear, when center is about 145°F. Let sit 3 minutes and serve.

CHAPTER 3

Soups for the Soul

W<small>HILE</small> soup may have been around since the beginning of cooking itself, and it may not cure the common cold or anything else, soup is good for the soul; it warms us and brings a feeling of comfort very few foods can match.

As we all know, soup is made by cooking various meats, vegetables, grains, beans, and pastas with a relatively large amount of liquid in a large pot. Some soups are seasoned with a variety of spices, including curry, basil, garlic, parsley, and, on the spicy side, red pepper and hot pepper sauce. Sometimes, when we want to be fancy, we like to dress up our soups with toppings, such as shredded cheese, bacon bits, seasoned croutons, a dollop of sour cream, or green onions. But no matter the ingredients, or how it's spiced or garnished, what we end up with is a nourishing, filling, and easily digested meal.

Soup has always been a favorite for tenderizing tough meat, feeding crowds, and stretching a dollar. In colonial times, this dish was especially popular, when thick concentrates known as "veal glue" or "pocket soup" were packed along by travelers. By the nineteenth century, canned and dehydrated soups became available. Today, numerous time-saving soups, including dry mixes, fill our grocery store shelves. But even though soup has become a common convenience food, we all know it's much more tasty and nutritious to make a fresh pot of soup from scratch.

And let's not forget stew—an assortment of foods cooked in liquid in a covered container—which, technically, too, is a soup. So, what's the difference between soup and stew? Well, some food historians say they are virtually the same, and that both descended from economical, easy, healthy, forgiving, and locally sourced foods. However, the test is not in the method or ingredients, but in how the two are served. Specifically, soup is supposed to be a starter to a meal, while stew is considered the main course. Nowadays, however, that rule is routinely broken, with soup serving as the meal, both in fast-food restaurants and upscale eateries, and especially at my house.

Soup has always had a special place on our family's dinner table. I remember my grandmother pulling out her favorite big pot from the pantry and making her "Soup for the Soul," a vegetable and beef concoction that more than three generations have enjoyed. Like so many African Americans, she never used a recipe. But along with all the expected ingredients, her soup was seasoned with a lot of love, which shone through and brought a lot of friends and families together. We lived in the middle of town in Halls, and people from our neighborhood used to come in droves when they knew Big Mama was preparing her famous soup. Sometimes she had to make a double batch just to feed everyone.

BIG MAMA'S SOUP FOR THE SOUL
YIELD: 8–10 SERVINGS

In addition to using inexpensive cuts of meat, Big Mama's soup always included fresh vegetables, potatoes, tomatoes, seasonings, spaghetti, and okra. Even today, I feel that a great pot of vegetable soup should always contain spaghetti and okra; that's just how Big Mama and my mom did it. To fully carry out our family tradition, finish this heartwarming soup with skillet cornbread.

1 (16-ounce) package frozen mixed vegetables
2 cups chopped okra, fresh or frozen

1 cup chopped onion

½ cup chopped green bell pepper

2 cups thinly sliced carrots

½ cup thinly sliced celery

Water or vegetable broth or stock (purchased, or use recipe
on pages 67–68), divided

2–3 cups cubed stew beef

Garlic powder to taste

1 (6-ounce) can tomato paste

3 (14.5-ounce) cans stewed tomatoes,
with liquid

1 (6-ounce) can tomato sauce

⅔ cup cooked regular or whole-wheat
spaghetti, drained

¼ cup ketchup

Salt and ground black pepper to taste

3 dashes red hot sauce (optional)

3 cups white potatoes, peeled and diced

1. In a medium pot, add mixed vegetables, okra, onion, bell
pepper, carrots, and celery. Add enough water to cover vegetables. Cook until tender. Drain; set aside.

2. In a separate large pot, add beef, cover with water by 2
inches, and gently boil until meat is tender, about 1 hour.
Season with garlic powder. Drain half the broth from beef
and reserve. Add tomato paste to the beef in the pot and
mix well. Stir in cooked vegetables.

3. To pot, add tomatoes, tomato sauce, spaghetti, ketchup, 1
cup reserved broth, salt, pepper, and hot sauce. Bring to a
boil; reduce heat and simmer, uncovered, 45 minutes. Add
diced potatoes and cook until tender, about 20 minutes.
Serve soup hot with Skillet Corn Bread (recipe on pages
128–129).

TIP: The hot sauce does not make the soup spicy; it just adds to the flavor.

BACON AND POTATO SOUP

YIELD: 8 SERVINGS

1 pound bacon, chopped into ½-inch dice
2 stalks celery, diced
1 cup chopped onion
2 garlic cloves, minced
8 medium potatoes, peeled and cubed
Chicken stock (purchased, or use recipe on
   pages 65–66)
3 tablespoons unsalted butter
¼ cup all-purpose flour
1 cup heavy cream
1 teaspoon dried tarragon
1 tablespoon chopped fresh cilantro
Seasoned salt to taste (purchased, or use
   recipe on pages 26–27)
Ground black pepper to taste

1. Cook the bacon in a large, heavy-bottomed Dutch oven until crisp. Remove cooked bacon from pan and set aside. Drain out all but ¼ cup of the bacon drippings.
2. Cook celery and onion in reserved bacon drippings until onion is translucent, about 3–5 minutes. Stir in garlic, and continue cooking for 1–2 minutes. Add potatoes and toss to coat. Sauté 3–4 minutes. Return bacon to the pan and add enough chicken stock to just cover the potatoes. Cover and simmer over medium heat until potatoes are tender, about 20 minutes. Set aside.
3. In a separate medium saucepan, melt butter over medium heat. Whisk in flour. Cook, stirring constantly, 1–2 minutes. Whisk in the heavy cream, tarragon, and cilantro. Bring the cream mixture to a boil and cook, stirring constantly, until thickened. Stir the cream mixture into the potato mixture. In a blender, puree about half of the soup, and return to the pan. Bring to a simmer; add seasoned salt and black pepper to taste. Serve hot.

HEARTY ITALIAN SAUSAGE SOUP

1 pound Italian sausage
½ cup chopped onion
1 clove garlic, minced
2 (14.5-ounce) cans chicken or vegetable stock
   (purchased, or use recipes on pages 65–68)
1 (14.5-ounce) can Italian-style stewed tomatoes,
   with liquid
1 cup sliced carrots
¼ teaspoon salt
¼ teaspoon ground black pepper
1 (14.5-ounce) can great northern beans,
   with liquid
2 small zucchini, cubed
1 cup spinach, packed, rinsed, and torn

1. In a stockpot, brown sausage with onion and garlic. Stir in stock, tomatoes, and carrots, and season with salt and black pepper. Reduce heat, cover, and simmer 15 minutes.
2. Stir in beans with their liquid and zucchini. Cover and simmer until zucchini is tender, 15 more minutes.
3. Remove pot from heat and stir in spinach. Allow to sit off of heat, uncovered, until spinach is completely wilted, about 5 minutes. Serve hot in mugs or bowls.

CREAM OF BROCCOLI SOUP

YIELD: 6 SERVINGS

5 tablespoons unsalted butter, divided
1 cup chopped onion
2 stalks celery, chopped
8 cups broccoli florets

3 cups chicken stock (purchased, or use recipe
  on pages 65–66)
3 tablespoons all-purpose flour
2 cups whole milk
Ground black pepper to taste

1. Melt 2 tablespoons butter in a medium stock pot over medium-high heat and sauté onion and celery until tender. Add broccoli and stock and bring to a boil. Cover, lower heat, and simmer 10 minutes.
2. Pour the soup into a blender, filling the pitcher no more than halfway full. (Be careful; it's really hot!) Hold down the lid with a folded kitchen towel and carefully start the blender, using a few quick pulses to get the soup moving before leaving it on to puree. Puree in batches until smooth and pour into a clean pot. Alternately, you can use a stick blender and puree the soup right in the cooking pot.
3. In a small saucepan, over medium heat, melt the remaining 3 tablespoons butter; stir in flour, and add milk. Stir until thick and bubbly and add to soup. Season with pepper and serve hot.

CHUNKY CHICKEN SOUP
YIELD: 6–8 SERVINGS

Nothing melts away the chill of winter like a nutritious bowl of homemade chicken soup. And making it is so simple. It always has been a favorite at my house, as it has been historically throughout the South.

3 medium boneless chicken breasts, cubed
2 cups chopped celery
1 cup chopped green onion
½ cup chopped white onion
3 garlic cloves, minced

Seasoned salt to taste (purchased, or use recipe
 on pages 26–27)
Ground black pepper to taste
1 cup sliced zucchini
2 cups peeled and diced white potatoes
2 carrots, sliced
1 teaspoon minced fresh chives
1 teaspoon rubbed sage
1 teaspoon dried thyme
½ teaspoon fresh minced rosemary
⅓ teaspoon red pepper (optional)
Chicken stock (purchased, or use recipe
 on pages 65–66)

1. Place chicken in a large pot with enough cold water to cover
   it. Add celery, green onion, white onion, garlic, seasoned
   salt, and black pepper. Cover and simmer slowly until
   chicken is fork-tender, about 1 hour.
2. Add zucchini, potatoes, carrots, chives, sage, thyme, rosemary, and red pepper. Add chicken stock if needed. Simmer
   until potatoes are done, about 15 minutes.
   Serve hot.

CHICKEN AND RICE SOUP

YIELD: ABOUT 2 QUARTS

4 pounds chicken pieces, skinned
1 cup chopped onion
2 stalks celery, thinly sliced
Seasoned salt to taste (purchased, or use recipe
 on pages 26–27)
Ground black pepper to taste
1 fresh bay leaf
Water

1 cup uncooked long-grain rice
1 cup diced carrots

1. In a medium pot, add chicken, onion, celery, seasoned salt, black pepper, and bay leaf, and add water to cover. Bring to a boil. Cover; reduce heat and simmer 45 minutes. Remove chicken and set aside, reserving stock.
2. Remove bay leaf from stock. Add rice and carrots; bring to a boil. Cover, reduce heat, and simmer until rice is tender, about 20 minutes.
3. De-bone chicken and cut into bite-sized pieces. Add chicken to stock; simmer until heated all the way through and serve.

SOUTHERN–STYLE CHILI

YIELD: 8–10 SERVINGS

It's really hard to agree on what makes a great chili. This southern favorite is as American as apple pie, and it is prepared with variations depending on region. Opinions differ on whether to add beans or not, to make it mild or spicy, and whether to add toppings. I certainly believe it's all a matter of personal preference. My favorite way of eating chili is with a sprinkling of grated cheese and green onion, and a side of oyster crackers.

2 pounds ground beef
1 cup chopped onion
4 garlic cloves, minced
2 tablespoons chili powder
2 teaspoons seasoned salt (purchased, or use recipe on pages 26–27)
1 teaspoon ground black pepper
2 teaspoons fresh oregano
4 (14.5-ounce) cans chopped stewed tomatoes, with liquid
1 (15-ounce) can tomato sauce

2 tablespoons red pepper sauce
1 (15-ounce) can kidney beans, with liquid
Grated Cheddar cheese (optional)
Chopped green onion (optional)
Oyster crackers for serving

1. In a large stockpot, combine ground beef, onion, and garlic. Cook and stir over medium heat until beef is brown. Drain.
2. Stir in chili powder, seasoned salt, black pepper, oregano, tomatoes, tomato sauce, and red pepper sauce. Heat to a boil; reduce heat to a simmer and cover. Cook, stirring occasionally, 20–30 minutes.
3. Stir in beans. Simmer, uncovered, for 20 minutes, stirring occasionally. Serve chili in bowls and top with cheese, chopped green onion, and oyster crackers.

TURKEY CHILI SOUP

YIELD: ABOUT 8–10 SERVINGS

3 tablespoons vegetable oil
1¼ cups chopped onion
1 cup chopped green bell pepper
2 (15-ounce) cans kidney beans, drained
1 (28-ounce) can crushed stewed tomatoes, with liquid
⅔ cup red wine
3 cups cubed cooked turkey
1 tablespoon chili powder
1 teaspoon minced cilantro leaves
1 teaspoon ground black pepper
1 teaspoon crushed red pepper (optional)
½ teaspoon seasoned salt (purchased, or use recipe on pages 26–27)
½ teaspoon garlic powder

1. Heat oil in large saucepan over medium heat. Add onion and green pepper; cook and stir 4–5 minutes or until vegetables are tender.
2. Stir in beans, tomatoes, wine, and turkey; mix well. Add chili powder, cilantro, black pepper, red pepper, seasoned salt, and garlic powder. Bring to a boil on high heat. Reduce heat to low and simmer, uncovered, 30 minutes. Serve hot in bowls.

HEARTY BEEF STEW WITH VEGETABLES

YIELD: ABOUT 8 SERVINGS

2 pounds lean stew beef

2–3 teaspoons vegetable oil

1 teaspoon seasoned salt, divided (purchased, or use recipe on pages 26–27)

1 cup chopped onions

1 can (10½ ounces) beef stock (purchased, or use recipe on page 66)

Hot water

3 cups peeled and diced white potatoes

2 cups diced carrots

1 stalk celery, cut into ½-inch pieces

1 teaspoon dried thyme

¼ teaspoon crushed red pepper flakes

1 (10-ounce) package frozen green peas, thawed

2 tablespoons all-purpose flour

⅓ cup cold water

Ground black pepper to taste

1. Cut the beef into small, bite-sized cubes. Heat oil in a large pot. Add beef, ½ teaspoon seasoned salt, and chopped on-

ions. Cook, turning frequently, over medium heat until the meat is browned on all sides and onion is tender, about 10–15 minutes. Drain off any excess fat.

2. Add beef stock and enough hot water to the pot until the liquid is about 1 inch above the beef. Cover, reduce heat to low, and simmer 1½–2 hours, or until the meat is tender.
3. Add the potatoes, carrots, celery, thyme, red pepper, and peas. Cover and cook, stirring occasionally, until vegetables are tender, about 20–30 minutes longer.
4. To thicken the stew, combine the flour with ⅓ cup cold water. Stir or whisk until smooth. Gently stir flour mixture into the pot a little at a time, using as much as needed to make the stew as thick as you like it.
5. Add black pepper and remaining ½ teaspoon of seasoned salt, if needed. Serve hot in bowls.

CAULIFLOWER CHEESE SOUP
YIELD: ABOUT 2 QUARTS

1 large head cauliflower, broken into bite-sized pieces
Water
1 teaspoon salt, divided
2 tablespoons minced onion
2 tablespoons unsalted butter, melted
2 tablespoons all-purpose flour
½ teaspoon salt
½ teaspoon ground black pepper
14–16 ounces chicken stock (purchased, or use recipe
   on pages 65–66)
3½ cups whole milk
2 cups grated Cheddar cheese
½ cup chopped fresh parsley (optional)

1. In a medium pot, add cauliflower and cover with water by ½ inch. Add salt and cook, covered, until tender. Drain and set aside.
2. In a medium pot over medium heat, sauté onion in butter until tender. Blend in flour, salt, black pepper, stock, and milk. Cook over medium heat, stirring constantly, until mixture starts to boil. Reduce to medium heat.
3. Add cheese and stir until it melts. Add cauliflower and parsley. Mix well and heat until it comes to a boil. Serve hot.

BIG MAMA'S NECK BONE SOUP
YIELD: 6–8 SERVINGS

When I was a young girl, Big Mama used to walk down to Larson Grocery Store and purchase the neck bones for this recipe. She would come back with enough bones to serve a small army. Some she used right away for soup, while the rest went into the freezer. Big Mama loved making this satisfying soup and we loved eating it. And, of course, it was always served with Skillet Corn Bread (recipe on pages 128–29).

> 4–5 pounds meaty pork neck bones
> Water
> 1 cup chopped yellow onion
> 3 garlic cloves, minced
> Seasoned salt (purchased, or use recipe on pages 26–27)
> Ground black pepper to taste
> 1 package (16-ounces) frozen mixed vegetables
> 2 (14-ounce) cans stewed tomatoes, with liquid
> 3 tablespoons red hot sauce (optional)
> 2 large bay leaves

1. Remove as much fat as possible from neck bones and place bones in a large pot over medium heat. Add enough water

to cover neck bones. Add onion, garlic, seasoned salt, and pepper. Cover pot and cook until the meat falls off the bones, about 2 hours.

2. Remove all bones, but do not drain pot. Chop meat into bite-sized size pieces, and add meat back to pot. Add mixed vegetables, stewed tomatoes, hot sauce, and bay leaves. Continue cooking over low heat until vegetables are tender, about 25 minutes. Remove bay leaves and serve hot.

TIP: You can also use beef neck bones for this recipe. Also, the hot sauce does not make this soup spicy; it just adds to the flavor.

EARL'S PINTO BEAN SOUP
YIELD: 6–8 SERVINGS

My husband, Earl, used to make this simple soup for our all-you-can-eat Sunday buffet when we owned our soul food restaurant, Earl's Southern Catering, in Milwaukee, Wisconsin. Beginning in the mid-1990s, we cooked southern-style food there for more than ten years, and Earl's soup was so popular that friends and family would come all the way from across town just to get a bowl.

During the days of slavery, pinto bean soup was made often by African American cooks who struggled to find inexpensive meals to prepare for their families. Today, still, dried pinto beans are a bargain. And they taste so good, we southerners now serve them in good economic times as well as bad.

The secret to properly seasoning this dish is to use high-quality smoked meat. This soup is filling enough for a meal, and is ideally served with Big Mama's Hot-Water Corn Bread (recipe on pages 129–30).

1 pound dried pinto beans, covered by 3 inches water
   and soaked overnight
4 ounces smoked meat (sausage, ham, etc.)
4 quarts cold water
¼ teaspoon ground red pepper (optional)

3 tablespoons vinegar
Ground black pepper to taste
Seasoned salt to taste (purchased, or use recipe
   on pages 26–27)

1. Drain beans. In a large pot, add beans, smoked meat, water, red pepper, vinegar, and pepper. Cook on high heat, covered, until beans come to a boil. Reduce to low heat and simmer, covered, until beans are very soft and liquid is soupy, about 2 hours, stirring often.
2. Stir in the seasoned salt. The finished dish should be thick and creamy. Serve hot.

TIP: Soaking the beans overnight helps reduce the cooking time. When serving, I also like to top this soup with chopped white onions.

OLD-FASHIONED CABBAGE SOUP
YIELD: 6–8 SERVINGS

Cabbage is one of the oldest-known vegetables and was, therefore, popular long before the cabbage diet craze. Pots containing this nutritious vegetable have been traced back to 4000 BC in China, which proves how long cabbage has been enjoyed. Over in China, cabbage today is often pickled and served over rice, which sounds pretty tasty to me. Here in Tennessee, where we also have a long history with cabbage, my grandmother used to make a meal with just cabbage, white potatoes, and skillet corn bread. Then there was her soup, which is a bit more complicated but also makes a quick, healthful, lip-smacking meal.

7 cups chopped green cabbage, cut into bite-sized pieces
1 quart water
Seasoned salt to taste (purchased, or use recipe
   on pages 26–27)
Ground black pepper to taste

2 (14-ounce) cans stewed tomatoes, with liquid
1 (14-ounce) can whole tomatoes, with liquid
⅔ cup chopped onion
½ cup chopped celery
½ cup chopped green bell pepper
2 garlic cloves, chopped
2 cups peeled and diced white potatoes

1. In a large pot, add cabbage, water, seasoned salt, and black pepper. Bring to a boil over high heat. Reduce to medium heat, and continue cooking 20 minutes.
2. Add stewed tomatoes, whole tomatoes, onion, celery, green bell pepper, and garlic. Stir in potatoes and cook until potatoes and cabbage are fork-tender, about 15 minutes. Serve hot.

BACON AND MUSHROOM SOUP
YIELD: 8 SERVINGS (ABOUT 2 QUARTS)

Mushroom soup was my mother's favorite, and I never really knew why—until now, when I just unearthed her recipe and had a bowlful with my more mature taste buds. This soup is so creamy! And the earthiness of the mushrooms really stands out. The Swiss cheese also adds a layer of flavor to this company-worthy dish.

10 strips bacon, cut into ½-inch dice
1 pound fresh cremini mushrooms, sliced
½ cup chopped onion
2 garlic cloves, minced
1 quart heavy whipping cream
14 ounces chicken stock (purchased, or use recipe on pages 65–66)
5 ounces shredded Swiss cheese
3 tablespoons cornstarch

½ teaspoon salt
½ teaspoon ground black pepper
2 tablespoons water

1. In a large saucepan, cook bacon over medium heat until crispy. Remove bacon and drain on paper towel, reserving 2 tablespoons drippings.
2. In a small saucepan, add drippings, mushrooms, and onion. Sauté 5 minutes. Add garlic and sauté 30 seconds. Stir in cream and stock. Bring to a boil, then lower heat to a simmer. Gradually add cheese and stir until melted. Remove pan from heat.
3. In a small bowl, combine cornstarch, salt, pepper, and water and stir until smooth. Bring soup back to a boil and stir in cornstarch mixture. Cook and stir until thickened, about 2–3 minutes. Garnish with bacon and serve hot.

CHEDDAR SEAFOOD CHOWDER

YIELD: ABOUT 4 SERVINGS

½ cup finely chopped onion
¼ cup unsalted butter
14 ounces seafood stock (purchased, or use recipe on pages 66–67)
1 cup peeled and cubed white potatoes
1 stalk celery, chopped
¼ cup chopped carrot
¼ cup Clamato juice
¼ teaspoon lemon pepper
⅛ teaspoon ground black pepper
¼ cup all-purpose flour
2 cups whole milk
2 cups shredded, sharp Cheddar cheese

1 (6-ounce) can crabmeat, drained, flaked with
   cartilage removed
1 cup cooked, peeled, and deveined medium shrimp

1. In a large saucepan, sauté onion in butter until tender. Stir
   in the stock, potato, celery, carrots, Clamato juice, lemon
   pepper, and black pepper. Bring to a boil. Reduce heat; cover
   and simmer until vegetables are tender, 15–20 minutes.
2. In a small bowl, whisk together flour and milk until
   smooth; add to soup. Bring to a boil; cook and stir for 2–3
   minutes, or until mixture thickens.
3. Reduce heat. Add cheese, crabmeat, and shrimp, and cook
   and stir until cheese is melted.
   Serve hot.

CREAMY TOMATO SOUP

YIELD: ABOUT 6 SERVINGS

*I first had this hearty soup when I was in high school on summer break, when
my mom would make it for my sister and me for lunch almost every weekday.
It just always seemed to hit the spot, and the more I had it, the more I fell in love
with it. For a smoother texture, feel free to puree the finished soup. I, however,
like it just the way it is.*

4 tablespoons unsalted butter
¼ cup chopped onion
¼ cup chopped celery
3 tablespoons all-purpose flour
3 cups whole milk
2 teaspoons white sugar
Salt and ground black pepper to taste
2 cans (14.5 ounces each) diced tomatoes, with liquid
Grated Parmesan cheese (optional)

1. In a large saucepan, heat butter over medium-low heat. Add onion and celery, and cook, stirring, until tender, about 5 minutes.
2. Stir flour into the vegetable mixture until well incorporated. Gradually stir in milk, sugar, salt, and black pepper. Continue to heat, stirring, until the mixture thickens and begins to boil.
3. In a separate saucepan, heat tomatoes until they just reach a simmer. Gradually add hot tomatoes to the milk mixture and stir constantly until soup reaches a boil. (For a smoother soup, puree in small batches in a blender. Return to pot and simmer 5 minutes.) Serve hot and garnished with freshly grated Parmesan cheese.

TURKEY AND VEGETABLE SOUP

YIELD: 6–8 SERVINGS

According to television's Dr. Mehmet Oz, turkey is loaded with tryptophan, a sleep-inducing amino acid. Turkey is also rich in potassium and loaded with zinc. Too, it's an excellent source of vitamin B12, which helps prevent the buildup of homocysteine, an amino acid that may decrease cognitive function. Turkey is definitely a delicious and healthy choice for the entire family.

3 medium turkey legs
Water
1 cup chopped celery
1 cup chopped onion
2 cloves garlic, chopped
Salt and black ground pepper to taste
2 cups stewed tomatoes, with liquid
2 cups peeled and diced white potatoes
½ cup sliced carrots
1 teaspoon minced fresh chives
1 teaspoon rubbed sage

1 teaspoon fresh thyme
1 teaspoon fresh rosemary
1 teaspoon poultry seasoning

1. Place turkey in a large pot over medium heat and cover with water. Add celery, onion, garlic, salt, and black pepper. Cover and simmer until turkey and vegetables are fork-tender, about 2 hours.
2. De-bone turkey and cut into bite-sized pieces. Discard bones and return turkey to pot with vegetables.
3. Add stewed tomatoes, potatoes, carrots, chives, sage, thyme, rosemary, and poultry seasoning, and cook until potatoes and carrots are tender, about 25 minutes. Serve hot.

HAM CHOWDER SOUP

YIELD: ABOUT 6 CUPS

2 cups diced and peeled white potatoes
3 cups cold water
½ cup sliced carrots
½ cup sliced celery
¼ cup chopped onion
Seasoned salt to taste (purchased, or use recipe
   on pages 26–27)
Ground black pepper to taste
¼ cup unsalted butter
¼ cup all-purpose flour
2 cups whole milk
8 ounces grated American cheese
1½ cups cooked, cubed ham

1. In a medium pot, bring to a boil potatoes, water, carrots, celery, onion, seasoned salt, and black pepper. Boil 10 minutes. Turn off heat and do not drain.

2. In a separate saucepan, melt butter and add flour. Stir until smooth. Gradually add milk and heat and stir until bubbles start to appear.
3. Combine milk mixture with cooked vegetables in pot. Add cheese and ham. Simmer, stirring, until cheese melts, 3–5 minutes. Serve immediately.

MEATBALL PARMESAN SOUP
YIELD: MAKES TWO 2-CUP SERVINGS

This easy soup is a take on Italian spaghetti and meatballs, with fresh vegetables sautéed in olive oil adding an additional layer of homemade flavor. And the recipe is perfectly portioned for one or two people.

1 tablespoon olive oil
1 cup sliced mushrooms (any kind)
3 cloves garlic, minced
3 cups beef stock
½ cup sliced baby-cut carrots
10 (1-inch) frozen Italian-style meatballs
½ cup rotini pasta (spiral-shaped)
½ teaspoon ground black pepper
2 cups chopped, fresh baby spinach
¼ cup shredded Parmesan cheese

1. Heat oil in a medium saucepan over medium heat until hot. Add mushrooms and garlic and cook until fragrant, about 30 seconds. Add stock and carrots; bring to a boil. Add meatballs, pasta, and black pepper, and return to a boil. Cover and reduce heat to medium-low.
2. Simmer 10–12 minutes, or until pasta is tender and meatballs are cooked through. Stir in spinach and serve topped with cheese.

WHITE BEAN AND HAM SOUP

YIELD: 4–6 SERVINGS

1 pound cannellini beans, soaked overnight covered
   by 3 inches water
4 cups water
½ cup chopped onion
2 carrots, peeled and sliced
3 garlic cloves, chopped
1 (14.5-ounce) can chopped stewed tomatoes, with liquid
1½ teaspoons Italian seasoning
10 ounces diced ham

1. Soak beans overnight. Drain and place beans in a slow
   cooker with 4 cups water, onion, carrots, garlic, stewed tomatoes, Italian seasoning, and ham.
2. Cook in slow cooker on high for about 6 hours. That's it—
   it's ready to serve! Great with Skillet Corn Bread (recipe on
   pages 128–129)

TIP: Soaking the beans overnight helps reduce the cooking time. I also like to
chop white onions on top of the beans when served.

ITALIAN MINESTRONE SOUP

YIELD: ABOUT 8 SERVINGS

¼ cup unsalted butter
¼ cup olive oil
2 large carrots, diced
2 cups chopped onion
2 celery stalks, thinly sliced
2 medium white potatoes, diced
1 leek, trimmed, washed, and thinly sliced

3 cups beef stock (purchased, or use recipe on
   page 66)
3 cups chicken stock (purchased, or use recipe
   on pages 65–66)
1 teaspoon salt
1 teaspoon ground black pepper
1 (19-ounce) can diced tomatoes, with liquid
1 zucchini, peeled and diced
1 (14-ounce) can red kidney beans, drained and rinsed
1 (14-ounce) can white kidney beans, drained and rinsed
½ cup dried spaghetti, broken into 1-inch pieces
Grated Parmesan cheese

1. Heat butter and oil in a large heavy pot or Dutch oven over
   medium heat. Add carrots, onion, celery, potatoes, and leek;
   sauté until vegetables are tender, stirring occasionally, for
   about 10–15 minutes.
2. Add stocks, salt, black pepper, tomatoes, and zucchini; simmer on low, stirring occasionally, for 30–35 minutes.
3. Add beans and spaghetti; simmer another 15 minutes. Serve
   hot and garnish each serving with fresh Parmesan.

CREAM OF CRABMEAT SOUP

YIELD: 6–8 SERVINGS

3 tablespoons unsalted butter
⅔ cup chopped onion
2 tablespoons all-purpose flour
2 cups clam juice or seafood stock (purchased, or use
   recipe on pages 66–67)
1 pound lump crabmeat, divided
2 cups half-and-half
1 teaspoon Old Bay seasoning
½ teaspoon garlic powder

½ teaspoon cayenne pepper (optional)
Seasoned salt to taste (purchased, or use recipe
    on pages 26–27)
Ground black pepper to taste
Dash of red hot sauce (optional)
1 teaspoon minced fresh parsley

1. In a large pot over medium heat, sauté the butter and onion
   until onion is tender but not brown. Add flour and stir
   2 minutes.
2. Whisk in clam juice. Bring to a boil, stirring constantly.
   Reduce heat and simmer 10 minutes. Add crabmeat, reserving a little for garnish, if desired.
3. Add half-and-half, Old Bay seasoning, garlic powder, cayenne, seasoned salt, black pepper, and red hot sauce. Mix
   well and simmer 5 minutes. Ladle soup into individual
   bowls and top with parsley and reserved crabmeat.

SIMPLE SPLIT PEA SOUP
YIELD: 6–8 SERVINGS

1 pound dry split peas
10 cups water
2 cups peeled and cubed white potatoes
2 cups chopped onion
1 cup chopped carrot
2 cups cubed cooked corned beef or ham
½ cup chopped celery
1 teaspoon dried marjoram
1 teaspoon poultry seasoning
1 teaspoon rubbed sage
1 teaspoon salt
1 teaspoon ground black pepper
½ teaspoon dried basil

Add all ingredients to a stock pot and bring to a gentle boil over medium-high heat. Reduce heat and simmer until vegetables are tender, about 60–90 minutes. Serve hot.

GARLIC AND ASPARAGUS SOUP

YIELD: ABOUT 4 SERVINGS

1 tablespoon olive oil
5 cloves garlic, thinly sliced
4 green onions, coarsely chopped
1½ pounds fresh asparagus, trimmed and
   coarsely chopped
2 (14-ounce) cans vegetable stock (purchased, or
   use recipe on pages 67–68)
Seasoned salt to taste (purchased, or use recipe
   on pages 26–27)
Ground black pepper to taste

1. Heat olive oil in a large saucepan over medium heat. Add garlic and green onions and cook, stirring occasionally, 3 minutes. Add asparagus and cook until slightly softened, about 2 more minutes.
2. Pour in vegetable stock and bring to a boil. Reduce heat and simmer until asparagus is tender, about 10 minutes. Turn off heat and allow soup to cool slightly.
3. Pour soup into a blender, filling no more than halfway full. Cover with a lid. Carefully start the blender by using a few quick pulses to get soup moving before leaving it on to puree. Puree in batches until smooth. Transfer soup back to saucepan and reheat. Season with salt and black pepper. Serve hot.

FUFU
(Pronounced FOO-FOO)
YIELD: 2–3 SERVINGS

Fufu is a dense dough ball used for dipping into stews and soups, and is a staple food of West and Central Africa. It was also very popular with America's antebellum slave population, who called the sweet potato nyami, *from a Fulani word meaning "to eat," or from the Twi word* anyinam, *referring to the true yam, which they remembered from back home.*

In the old days, slaves boiled starchy root vegetables, usually sweet potatoes, then pounded them with a large mortar and pestle to form a thick paste. The paste was rolled into a ball and served with roasted meat, and particularly with soup and stew. And it's still good with those dishes. This recipe is made without the pounding and is therefore a much simpler version of the way slaves prepared Fufu.

There is much confusion over yams and sweet potatoes, which are different tubers and are only distantly related. The yam is a starchy, edible root vegetable native to Asia and Africa, and its flesh can be colored white, yellow, purple, or pink. A mature yam can weigh up to 10 pounds, and over 95 percent of the international yam crop grows in West Africa. The vegetable is important to Nigeria, in particular, a country that produces 75 percent of the world's yams, and where festivals honoring the harvest involve feasting and carnival-like festivities.

Here in the United States, we eat the sweet potato, which is really not a potato, and which came here from Central America. Sweet potatoes, like yams, are tubers that can also vary in color from white to orange to purple. Aside from being much smaller than yams, sweet potatoes have less starch, are moister, and much sweeter. But the main difference between the two is that they are from totally different plant families.

In the 1930s, Louisiana State University researchers developed an exceptionally sweet variety of sweet potato and decided to distinguish it from the others by marketing it as a "Louisiana yam." Soon, many markets began to advertise sweet potatoes as yams—and to everyone's surprise, the name stuck.

1 large sweet potato (about 2 cups)
1 cup water

3–4 tablespoons unsalted butter
1 large egg
1 tablespoon, plus 2 teaspoons evaporated milk
½ cup finely grated onion
Pinch of garlic salt
All-purpose flour

1. Peel and cut sweet potato into small pieces. In a saucepan, boil pieces in water until tender, about 20 minutes. Drain off the water and mash until smooth. Set aside.
2. In a medium skillet, melt butter. While butter is melting, in a small bowl, mix together the cooked sweet potato, egg, milk, onion, and garlic salt.
3. Roll mixture into 2-inch balls. If the mixture is too wet to hold the shape of a ball, add a little flour. Fry balls over medium heat in hot butter until brown. Serve with your favorite soup.

WHY WE LOVE HOMEMADE STOCK

Is there anything more satisfying than the wonderful smell of stock simmering on the stove? I grew up with the aromas of a simmering pot of beef or chicken wafting throughout the kitchen, where homemade stock always was the base for meat sauces, soups, and purees. As it has been done in my family for generations, I prepare my stock today inexpensively from fresh, or maybe not-so-fresh, vegetables and a hen carcass, or maybe a ham bone or meat trimmings. In a pinch, I do buy meat specifically for stock, but typically I make it with something left over. Herbs and spices, of course, always round out the flavor. And what I really love about making my own stock is that I control the salt content.

So what's the difference between stock and broth? Well, stock is made from more bony animal parts, while broth is typically made out of the actual meat. Because of the gelatin that leeches from all those bones, stock has a richer flavor and a fuller mouth feel. (Because they contain no meat, vegetable broths and stocks are the same thing.)

The main idea in preparing stock is to draw all the goodness out of the vegetables, meat, and seasonings into the liquid. This is done by a long and gentle simmering process. And I don't believe there is really a wrong way to make it, just as long as you include the base ingredients of meat or meat bones, vegetables, herbs, and spices. With this winning combination, anyone can make a great pot of homemade stock.

CHICKEN STOCK

YIELD: ABOUT 2 QUARTS

I make this stock because it adds depth of flavor and a richness that "dresses up" my corn bread dressing. It's also a good base for soups and gravies.

2 pounds chicken backs and necks
8–10 cups water
1 cup chopped onion
1 cup chopped green bell pepper
3 celery stalks, with leaves, chopped
2 carrots, sliced
1 tablespoon chopped fresh parsley
1 teaspoon seasoned salt (purchased, or use
   recipe on pages 26–27)
1 teaspoon ground black pepper
2 tablespoons rubbed sage
2 tablespoons poultry seasoning
1 teaspoon minced fresh chives

1. In a large pot over medium heat, combine chicken and water. Bring to a boil. Skim off fat or residue that rises to the top. Reduce heat and partially cover pot. Simmer 30 minutes.
2. Add the onion, bell pepper, celery, carrots, parsley, seasoned salt, black pepper, sage, poultry seasoning, and chives. Simmer, covered, 2–3 hours longer.
3. Remove chicken from stock and remove meat from bones. Discard bones. Strain stock through a fine sieve, pressing

on vegetables to extract juices. Cool to room temperature before refrigerating.

BEEF STOCK

YIELD: 3–4 CUPS

¼ cup vegetable oil
2 teaspoons salt
2 teaspoons ground black pepper
3 pounds beef bones (shank or beef neck bones)
1 cup diced onion
1 cup diced green bell pepper
4 quarts water

1. Heat oil in large pot over high heat. Sprinkle bones with salt and pepper. Add bones, onion, and bell pepper to pot. Sauté until bones, onion, and pepper are browned, turning often, about 20 minutes. Add water and bring to boil.
2. Reduce heat to medium-low and simmer uncovered until stock is reduced to 3–4 cups, about 3½ hours. Strain stock through a fine sieve, pressing on vegetables and beef to extract juices. Discard bones and vegetables. Refrigerate, uncovered, until cold, then cover and keep chilled.

TIP: This stock can be made 3 days ahead. Spoon off and discard all fat before using. Also, beef neck bones are an inexpensive meat to use for this stock.

SEAFOOD STOCK

YIELD: APPROXIMATELY 1 QUART

This stock adds richness to just about any seafood recipe that calls for liquid. When making this recipe, you can also add fish bones, fish ends, and skins, which will intensify the flavor.

2 tablespoons vegetable oil

1 pound shrimp shells

2 cups chopped yellow onion

2 carrots, chopped

3 celery stalks, chopped

2 cloves garlic, chopped

Cold water

⅓ cup tomato paste

1 tablespoon kosher salt or regular salt

1½ teaspoons freshly ground black pepper

2 sprigs fresh thyme, with stems

1. Heat the oil in a stockpot over medium heat. Add the shrimp shells, onion, carrots, and celery and sauté for 10 minutes, or until lightly browned. Add the garlic and cook 2 more minutes.
2. Add 1½ quarts of water, tomato paste, salt, pepper, and thyme. Bring to a boil; then reduce the heat and simmer for 1 hour.
3. Strain through a sieve, pressing the solids. There should be approximately 1 quart of stock. If too strong-tasting, add more water.

VEGETABLE STOCK

YIELD: ABOUT 3 QUARTS

1 tablespoon unsalted butter

1 tablespoon olive oil

1 cup chopped onion

2 large carrots, chopped

2 parsnips, coarsely chopped

2 stalks celery, chopped

1 bunch red or green Swiss chard, washed thoroughly
    and chopped into 1-inch pieces

3 quarts water, plus 2 cups

5 sprigs fresh thyme
5 sprigs fresh parsley
1 dried bay leaf

1. In a medium stock pot over medium-high heat, melt butter and olive oil. Add onion and cook until translucent, stirring constantly, about 3–5 minutes. Add carrots, parsnips, and celery and cook until tender, about 15 minutes.
2. Add the chard to the vegetable mixture. Add all of water, thyme, parsley, and bay leaf. Bring to a boil; then reduce heat and simmer 1 hour.
3. Remove from heat. Strain stock through a fine sieve, pressing on vegetables to extract juices. Discard vegetables. Cool to room temperature and refrigerate until ready to use.

SOUP AND STOCK FREEZING TIPS

Most soups freeze well, however there are a few freezing tips for you to keep in mind.

- Always cool soup down before freezing. And for maximum freshness, freeze in an airtight freezer-safe container.
- To retain flavor, do not freeze soup for more than three months.
- Do not freeze soup that contains pasta; the pasta will get mushy. Cook pasta in soup just before serving.
- Soups made with cream and potatoes should not be frozen. These ingredients can become grainy when frozen and then unthawed.
- The thawing process will be faster if you freeze in small batches.
- Never fill containers or freezer bags to the top. Instead, always fill about one-half to two-thirds full from the top to allow enough space to remove excess air.
- Many recipes call for small amounts of broth, so don't freeze your broth in large, hard-to-defrost containers; ice cube trays are perfect for the job.

CHAPTER 4

Barbecuing and Grilling in the South

HUMANS have been cooking over open flames since we first learned to corral fire, or even before, when wildfires served as stoves. It's only relatively recently that we do not have to worry about what meat we will cook, the fuel we will use, and the structures we will use to make it all work. That brings us to barbecue, the art of slowly roasting over controlled heat, which results in meat that's smoky, juicy, and fall-apart tender.

Without argument, barbecue as we know it is an invention of the American South, and it is also closely tied with African American cooking. So exactly how was southern barbecue invented? Food historians have several theories, but most think that when the Spanish landed in the Caribbean they used the word *barbacoa* to refer to the natives' method of slow-cooking meat over a wooden platform. By the nineteenth century, the culinary technique was well established in the American South, where pigs were plentiful, and pork became the primary meat on southern pits. Since barbecue during this time was still mostly done on open fires, it was ideal for cooking large quantities of food all at once, and it became the go-to menu item for large gatherings, such as church festivals, family reunions, and neighborhood picnics.

On antebellum plantations, the jobs of slaughtering, preparing pits and fires, and doing the actual barbecuing fell on the shoulders of slaves. In the early twentieth century, there was a mass migration of

African Americans from southern to northern cities. When these folks moved they took their cooking skills, methods, and recipes with them, and by the 1950s, black-owned barbecue joints were popping up in nearly every city in America. So, in addition to fried chicken, collard greens, and corn bread, barbecue became labeled as "soul food." All this explains why African Americans in today's South own so many successful barbecue restaurants and why there is a very strong bond between barbecue and the African American community.

Grilling is a little different from barbecuing in that it involves searing meat quickly, and with a significant amount of direct, radiant heat. A fat steak or a delicate piece of fish, for example, are best cooked on a grill because they require short cooking times to lock in the juices. Other foods perfect for grilling include hamburgers, hot dogs, shellfish, poultry, and vegetables. To keep meat and vegetables from drying out over a grill's intense heat, it's usually best to brush on a thin sauce or marinade during the cooking process.

Today, grilling and barbecuing are more popular than ever, and a hungry southerner can sniff some out in almost any American city. But even though most places now sell their own, barbecue will always be associated with the South, where this distinctly American cooking technique began, and where it continues to be refined and evolve.

Growing up in Tennessee, I remember my dad doing all the barbecuing, which usually meant only grilling ribs and chicken. Then I married Earl, a barbecue chef who does the whole nine yards, including barbecuing, grilling, and smoking. Equipped with an all-steel, barrel-type barbecue pit and a wildly popular barbecue sauce he keeps secret, Earl knows how to coax the flavor out of a piece of meat. Many people claim Earl's barbecue is the best they've ever had. One reason for this notoriety is that he takes his time to do things right, including barbecuing the old-fashioned way, with charcoal and hickory wood chips.

Earl taught himself how to barbecue and smoke meat, and he lights up his grill a few times a month when the weather is nice, and for holidays all year long. And although he sometimes caters large events, today's barbecues are mostly for family and friends.

During the ten years we lived in Milwaukee, where we ran Earl's Southern Bar-B-Que, we started a tradition of barbecuing at our home on New Year's Day, even if there was snow on the ground, which there usually was. Needless to say, we were the only family in that neighborhood who made our own New Year's barbecue.

HOW I SMOKE MEAT ON A CHARCOAL GRILL
BY BARBECUE CHEF EARL HARRELL

I like to smoke meat that's already barbecued or grilled, which adds another layer of flavor and makes the meat more tender. Smoking can take anywhere from 20 minutes to several hours, depending on the level of smokiness you want to achieve. If you're new to smoking meat, first start with something simple, such as barbecued chicken or pork shoulder. And for best flavor, use hickory wood chips.

Here are my tips to smoking any kind of cooked or grilled meat on a charcoal grill:

1. Use a one-level grill with about 20 inches of cooking space.
2. Place 3 charcoal briquettes close together inside the grill's charcoal pan. Squirt with liquid charcoal lighter fluid until the charcoals are soaking wet. Light charcoal; let turn a white-ash color, about 15–20 minutes.
3. Knock the ashes off the coals with tongs.
4. Take a handful of hickory chips and place them directly on top of the hot charcoals. (Because wet wood chips take longer to start smoking, I do not soak my wood chips.) Once the chips begin to smoke, place the grill grate or rack on top of the charcoal.
5. Place the cooked meat about 3 inches apart on the rack. If you're smoking pork shoulder or chopped meat, first place it in a wire grilling basket. Close grill top.
6. Smoke the meat until the hickory chips stop smoking, about 15–20 minutes.
7. If you want a deeper smoke flavor, repeat the process.

A TIP FROM EARL: For safety's sake, have a bottle filled with water handy on the side. This is especially important if the wind is high, which might cause the chips to catch on fire.

BARBECUED AND SMOKED PORK SHOULDER

YIELD: 12–15 PULLED-PORK SANDWICHES (OR 10 ENTRÉE SERVINGS).
RECIPE COURTESY OF EARL HARRELL.

This is Earl's much-acclaimed recipe for barbecuing a pork shoulder or roast and smoking it after it's chopped. We usually serve it in Barbecued Pork Sandwiches (recipe on page 74). Preparing it properly takes up to 8 hours. That seems like a long time, but it's a process that produces meat that's incomparably moist, tender, and full of smoky flavor. And Earl is always showered with so many compliments he certainly doesn't mind the time it takes to make.

1 (5–6-pound) pork shoulder or pork butt roast. (Pork should not have a lot of fat on it, and it should be firm with a pink color. Always make sure the meat is fresh, and that it is not past the expiration date.)
Salt and pepper, or Dry Rub for Pork (recipe follows)
Barbecue sauce (purchased, or Basic Barbecue Sauce recipe on page 82)

Equipment and Supplies:
One-level barbecue grill with 20 inches of cooking space
70 charcoal briquettes
Charcoal lighter fluid
A long (at least 15-inch) metal object to stir charcoal
Aluminum foil for wrapping the meat

1. At each end of the inside of a grill stack 35 pieces of charcoal, for a total of 70 pieces.
2. Pour on enough charcoal lighter fluid to cover the top of each pile. Let sit 2 minutes, then light charcoal. Allow charcoal to burn until edges turn to white ash, about 10–15 minutes. Put grill grate on top of charcoal.
3. Season meat with salt and pepper or dry rub. Wrap the meat loosely in aluminum foil (to speed up cooking and prevent burning).
4. Place the wrapped shoulder in the center of the inside grill

rack; do not put directly over the pile of charcoal. (The drippings will cause the flame to flare up and burn the meat, and centering the meat also allows even cooking.) Close grill cover and cook 5 hours, maintaining a grill temperature of 375°F–425°F.

5. After 5 hours, the shoulder should be fork-tender and easily pulled apart. If more cooking is needed, repeat step 2, but only add about 15 pieces of charcoal on each side; then relight the charcoal with the lighter fluid, etc. Let pork cook an additional 1–2 hours.

6. When the pork is fork-tender, carefully remove it from grill and transfer to a large pan or baking sheet. Let sit until cool enough to handle. Remove and discard fat; chop into bite-sized pieces.

7. Smoke the chopped meat using the instructions above in "How I Smoke Meat on a Charcoal Grill." After chopped meat is smoked, pour on your favorite barbecue sauce. Cooked shoulder can be frozen up to 4 months.

DRY RUB FOR PORK

YIELD: ABOUT ½ CUP. RECIPE COURTESY OF EARL HARRELL.

Earl believes that this no-fuss rub brings out the flavor of any cut of pork. For maximum penetration, rub meat with seasoning mix and let sit in the refrigerator at least 4–6 hours.

2 tablespoons paprika
2 tablespoons light brown sugar
2 tablespoons seasoned salt (purchased, or use
   recipe on pages 26–27)
2 tablespoons ground black pepper
1 teaspoon ground red pepper
1 teaspoon dry mustard
1 teaspoon dried parsley

Blend all ingredients in a small bowl. Rub on pork and let set for several hours. Store leftover dry rub at room temperature in an airtight container for up to 6 months.

TENNESSEE-STYLE BARBECUED PORK SANDWICHES

YIELD: 4–5 SANDWICHES. RECIPE COURTESY OF EARL HARRELL.

Earl reminds us that in west Tennessee, it's traditional to add coleslaw to a barbecued pork sandwich. And we also like the tang of chopped onions.

1–1½ pounds pulled pork, shredded (purchased, or use recipe above, making either smoked or unsmoked meat that has not been covered with sauce)
½–1 cup barbecue sauce (purchased, or use recipe on page 82)
5 split hamburger buns
Southern-Style Coleslaw (recipe follows) (optional)
Chopped onions (optional)

1. In a medium saucepan, mix pulled pork with barbecue sauce; heat until hot.
2. Divide pork among buns, using about 2 heaping tablespoons meat for each.
3. Top meat with 2 teaspoons of slaw, then with as much chopped onions as you like. Serve hot.

SOUTHERN-STYLE COLESLAW

YIELD: 6 CUPS

Like most barbecue lovers from west Tennessee, Earl and I eat pork sandwiches with coleslaw. Some people serve it on the side, but I usually place about 2 teaspoons on the inside of the top sandwich bun. And folks up in Wisconsin love this coleslaw, too. When Earl and I were catering for the Milwaukee Bucks, this recipe was always on the menu.

This is an old recipe I got from my mother, and it's the real deal. What makes this coleslaw southern? Aside from sugar and a healthy dose of mayonnaise, the main reason is that the cabbage, onions, and carrots are sliced with a hand grater; a true Tennessee-style coleslaw does not begin with cabbage bought precut from the store. Hand-grating vegetables just tastes fresher, and for some reason the dressing adheres better.

1½ cups mayonnaise or salad dressing
2 tablespoons white sugar
1 tablespoon freshly squeezed lemon juice
1 teaspoon salt
1 teaspoon ground black pepper
4 cups grated cabbage
⅓ cup grated onions
⅓ cup grated carrots

1. In a medium bowl, combine mayonnaise, sugar, lemon juice, salt, and black pepper.
2. Stir in cabbage, onions, and carrots. Mix well. Cover and chill up to 1 day.

TIP: You can use a food processor to grate the vegetables. This recipe can also be halved.

EARL'S FAMOUS BARBECUED SPARERIBS

YIELD: 4–6 SERVINGS. RECIPE COURTESY OF EARL HARRELL.

This is Earl's fail-proof rib recipe, and it is another menu item the Milwaukee Bucks basketball team requested every time we catered for them.

2 slabs pork spareribs
½–⅔ cup vinegar, depending on your taste

Seasoned salt to taste (purchased, or use recipe
  on pages 26–27)
Ground black pepper to taste
Garlic powder, enough to season each side
1 tablespoon paprika
1 teaspoon dry mustard
1 teaspoon cayenne pepper (optional)
Barbecue sauce (purchased, or use Basic Barbecue
  Sauce recipe on page 82)

1. Put ribs in a large pan and pour vinegar over both sides of ribs. Season both sides of ribs well with salt, pepper, garlic powder, paprika, dry mustard, and cayenne pepper. Cover and refrigerate overnight.
2. Wrap each slab separately in aluminum foil; set aside. Heat a gas grill to medium heat, or heat a charcoal grill until the coals turn the color of white ash. Place a rack 6 inches above heat source.
3. Place wrapped ribs, meaty side down, on grill directly over heat source. Cover and let cook until slightly tender, about 50–60 minutes.
4. Discard foil and place ribs directly on grill grate over heat source. Cover and cook until tender, about 20–30 more minutes, turning and basting both sides every 10 minutes. When ribs are tender, remove from grill, slice into single bones, and serve.

A TIP FROM EARL: I like to barbecue with charcoal because that's what I'm used to using and because charcoal imparts more flavor than a gas grill. I'm also a fan of using an aluminum foil wrap on ribs because it helps the meat cook faster, and it locks in the juices and keeps the meat from drying out. If you want to add even more flavor, smoke the cooked ribs following the instructions for smoking meat on a charcoal grill on page 71.

BARBECUED PORK RIB TIPS

YIELD: 4–6 SERVINGS. RECIPE COURTESY OF EARL HARRELL.

A rib tip is the cut of meat left over when pork spareribs are trimmed St. Louis-style. The resulting "tips" are short and flat, and usually don't have much bone, but they do have cartilage and a hefty morsel of meat. To cut your own, purchase packages of single strips of short ribs, then slice them into 2-inch rib tips.

Rib tips are usually served as an appetizer, but they can certainly be the main course. Just add your favorite side dish for a complete meal. I like buying rib tips because they're less messy to eat than a full rib bone, and children also love the smaller pieces.

½ cup ketchup
2 tablespoons brown sugar
2 tablespoons Worcestershire sauce
2 tablespoons red hot sauce
1 tablespoon cider vinegar
1 teaspoon garlic powder
¼ teaspoon mustard powder

4 pounds pork rib tips
Seasoned salt to taste (purchased, or use recipe
   on pages 26–27)
Ground black pepper to taste

1. Make sauce: In a small saucepan over medium heat, stir together the ketchup, brown sugar, Worcestershire sauce, hot sauce, vinegar, garlic powder, and mustard powder. Bring to a simmer; then remove from heat. Cool slightly.
2. Grill rib tips: Preheat grill to medium heat. Season rib tips with salt and pepper. Place on grill directly over heat source and cook until the outside has browned, 20–30 minutes. Reduce heat or move meat to a cooler part of the grill. Brush

with sauce and continue grilling until rib tips are tender, about 20 more minutes. Serve with remaining sauce.

A TIP FROM EARL: Add more barbecue flavor by smoking these rib tips after cooking. (Instructions for smoking meat on a charcoal grill on page 71.)

BARBECUED TURKEY LEGS

YIELD: 6 SERVINGS

Lean, protein-packed turkey needn't only be served on holidays. Easy-to-handle turkey legs, in particular, can be served any time of year. Whole turkey legs are tasty on their own as an entrée, but are also large enough to slice into sandwiches. For a big flavor punch, I like to brush on a little barbecue sauce toward the end of cooking.

1 cup finely chopped onion
½ cup finely chopped celery
1 tablespoon unsalted butter
1 cup water
1 (8-ounce) can tomato sauce
½ cup ketchup
3 tablespoons brown sugar
2 tablespoons yellow prepared mustard
1 tablespoon Worcestershire sauce
½ teaspoon garlic powder

6 turkey legs
Seasoned salt to taste (purchased, or use recipe
    on pages 26–27)
Ground black pepper to taste

1. Make sauce: In a saucepan, sauté onion and celery in butter until soft. Add water, tomato sauce, ketchup, brown sugar,

mustard, Worcestershire sauce, and garlic powder. Mix well. Bring to a boil; remove from heat. Set aside.

2. Grill turkey legs: Preheat a charcoal grill to medium heat. Season turkey legs with salt and pepper. Place turkey on grill directly over heat source. Cover and cook, turning a few times, until nearly done, about 30–45 minutes, depending on size.

3. Begin basting with sauce and make sure to watch closely to assure that the turkey does not burn. Grill until done, when the meat's internal temperature reaches 165°F. Serve warm.

TIP: You can also put a dry rub on the turkey legs before cooking (see recipe on pages 73–74).

MAPLE-GLAZED BARBECUE CHICKEN BREASTS
YIELD: 4 SERVINGS

¼ cup maple syrup
3 tablespoons brown sugar
1 tablespoon tomato paste
1 tablespoon red wine vinegar
1 teaspoon salt, divided
1 clove garlic, minced
½ teaspoon chopped fresh parsley
4 boneless, skinless chicken breast halves
¼ teaspoon ground black pepper

1. Make glaze: In a small bowl stir together maple syrup, brown sugar, tomato paste, red wine vinegar, ¼ teaspoon salt, garlic, and parsley. Mix well and set aside.

2. Barbecue the chicken: Prepare a gas or charcoal grill to medium heat. Season chicken with remaining ¾ teaspoon

salt and black pepper. Brush chicken generously with glaze. Place chicken 4–6 inches directly over heat. Cover grill.

3. Cook until juices run clear, turning once and brushing a few times with glaze, about 8–10 minutes. Serve hot.

SOUTHERN–STYLE BARBECUED CHICKEN

YIELD: 8 SERVINGS

When I was growing up in the 1960s, on weekends my dad did like many black families and barbecued a lot of chicken because it was inexpensive. Other economical dishes were the typical sides of collard greens and sweet potatoes. This "soul food" meal tasted so fantastic that it became a staple not only for those with lean bank accounts but also for those with a few dollars in their pockets. Today, still, chicken won't break your budget. And that's all the more reason to light up the pit and throw on a few fryers, which are fantastic when jazzed up with a simple tomato-based Memphis-style sauce. The following barbecue sauce is the one my dad used.

1½ cups white sugar
1½ cups ketchup
¼ cup water
¼ cup lemon juice
¼ cup cider vinegar
¼ cup Worcestershire sauce
3 tablespoons, plus 1 teaspoon chili powder
2 tablespoons, plus 2 teaspoons prepared yellow
    mustard
1 teaspoon seasoned salt (purchased or use recipe
    on pages 26–27)
½ teaspoon red crushed pepper flakes (optional)

2 broiler/fryer chickens (3½–4 pounds each), cut up

1. Make sauce: In a large saucepan, combine sugar, ketchup, water, lemon juice, cider vinegar, Worcestershire sauce, chili powder, mustard, salt, and red pepper flakes. Let the sauce come to a boil; then reduce heat and simmer, uncovered, for 15 minutes. Divide sauce between 2 bowls.
2. Grill chicken: Over medium heat, cook chicken directly over heat source, covered, for 40 minutes, turning several times. Coat chicken with sauce from 1 bowl and grill until juices run clear, about 10 minutes longer. Remove to a platter and serve with sauce from remaining bowl.

BARBECUED BOLOGNA
YIELD: 6 SERVINGS

As a youngster, I used to walk a few blocks with my older sister to the Larson Grocery Store, where we bought bologna slices that we quickly gobbled up. Years later, my dad starting grilling bologna, and he would slather on barbecue sauce and end up with a delicious and inexpensive treat for the entire family. They say that when you grow up eating a lot of something, when you get older you either love it or you hate it. Well, I still love bologna.

6 slices all-meat bologna, ¼-inch thick
Basic Barbecue Sauce (recipe follows)

1. Prepare a grill for high heat. Grill the bologna directly over heat until both sides start to brown, about 2–4 minutes total.
2. Brush each side of bologna generously with barbecue sauce. Continue grilling until the sauce sticks to the bologna, another 2 minutes on each side. Serve warm.

TIP: I like to use good-quality all-meat bologna. And barbecued bologna is also great served as a sandwich with Southern-Style Coleslaw (recipe on pages 74–75).

BASIC BARBECUE SAUCE

This is an all-purpose sauce that's good on chicken, pork, and beef.

½ cup ketchup
2 tablespoons brown sugar
2 tablespoons Worcestershire sauce
2 tablespoons red hot sauce
1 tablespoon cider vinegar
1 teaspoon garlic powder
¼ teaspoon mustard powder
¼ teaspoon salt
¼ teaspoon ground black pepper
⅛ teaspoon red pepper flakes

In a small saucepan over medium heat, bring all ingredients to a boil; then lower to a simmer and cook 2 minutes. Remove from heat; cool slightly before brushing on meat.

EASY GRILLED SALMON

YIELD: 4 SERVINGS

3 tablespoons unsalted butter, melted
1 tablespoon lemon juice
1 tablespoon white wine vinegar
¼ teaspoon grated lemon peel
¼ teaspoon garlic salt
¼ teaspoon salt
4 (6-ounce) salmon steaks

1. Make marinade: In a small bowl, combine the butter, lemon juice, white wine vinegar, lemon peel, garlic salt, and salt. Mix well. Generously brush both sides of the

salmon with mixture and cook right away or refrigerate up
to 30 minutes.

2. Grill the salmon: Prepare a grill for high heat. Place mari-
nated salmon on an oiled grill directly over hot coals. Cover
lightly with a piece of foil or the pit cover. Cook until
salmon is just cooked through and flakes easily with a fork,
6–8 minutes per side, depending on thickness. Turn only
once and baste frequently. Serve warm.

ALL-AMERICAN GRILLED HAMBURGERS

YIELD: 4 SERVINGS

*Food historians believe the modern hamburger originated in the eighteenth cen-
tury in the German city of Hamburg, where beef was minced and combined
with spices, then formed into patties to make what was called a Hamburg steak.
These early burgers (made without buns) were considered a real treat, but were
quite costly because of the high quality and price of Hamburg beef. Fortunately,
today's hamburgers are affordable. And this old-time favorite is an essential part
of American family picnics and kids' parties, and they are, of course, hot items at
casual and fast-food restaurants.*

*Ground beef is the largest beef item sold by volume. It's made from pieces
left over after trimming roasts and steaks, and can vary from 70 to 95 percent
lean. Ground chuck, on the other hand, is cut from the front beef shoulders,
and it's 85 percent lean. I usually select whatever is on sale. And on occasion I
combine ground beef and chuck, which provides a good balance of fat and flavor
for meat loaf. Whichever beef you decide to purchase, both cuts of meat are budget-friendly and make delicious hamburgers.*

1 pound lean ground beef or ground chuck
1 tablespoon Worcestershire sauce
1 teaspoon garlic powder
Seasoned salt to taste (purchased, or use recipe
    on pages 26–27)
Ground black pepper to taste

1 egg

¼ cup bread crumbs

2 tablespoons olive oil

4 hamburger buns

Mayonnaise (purchased, or use Basil Pesto Spread
   or Blue Cheese Spread, recipes follow)

4 lettuce leaves

Sliced onions

Sliced tomatoes

Dill pickle slices

1. Preheat grill for medium heat. In a medium bowl, combine the ground beef, Worcestershire sauce, garlic powder, salt, pepper, and egg. Mix well. Add the bread crumbs and mix well again.
2. Form seasoned beef into 4 patties. Brush both sides of each patty with olive oil.
3. Place the patties on the grill 4–6 inches from heat source. Cover grill and cook until no longer pink inside, about 5 minutes per side.
4. Place buns over coals and grill until lightly toasted, about 30–60 seconds. Serve meat on buns that are spread with mayonnaise or your choice of sauce. Top patties with lettuce, sliced onions, tomato, and dill pickle slices.

BASIL PESTO SPREAD

YIELD: 6–8 SERVINGS

This garden-fresh spread is good with cold sandwiches as well as hamburgers. It starts with a pesto concentrate that's mixed with mayonnaise to create something really different and delicious. You have to try it.

2 cups fresh basil leaves

2 large whole garlic cloves

½ cup freshly grated Parmesan cheese
2 tablespoons freshly grated Romano cheese
¼ cup pine nuts
½ cup good-quality olive oil, plus additional
   if needed
Salt and freshly ground black pepper to taste
½ cup mayonnaise

1. Combine basil, garlic, cheeses, and pine nuts in a food processor or blender. Process until smooth. With the machine running, slowly drizzle in ½ cup olive oil. Season with salt and pepper. Continue until blending desired consistency, adding more olive oil if needed. Let stand 5 minutes.
2. In a small bowl, mix mayonnaise with 1 teaspoon pesto. Taste, and for stronger flavor, add more pesto ½ teaspoon at a time. Spread on sandwich buns.

TIP: To store the pesto, fill a jar almost to the top. Drizzle a few teaspoons olive oil over the pesto then seal the jar closed. This will keep in the refrigerator for about 3–4 weeks.

BLUE CHEESE SPREAD

YIELD: ABOUT 1⅔ CUPS

This is another spread that's good on any sandwich.

1 cup crumbled blue cheese
⅔ cup mayonnaise
⅛ teaspoon ground black pepper

In a small bowl, combine blue cheese, mayonnaise, and black pepper; mix well. Spread heaping amount on hamburger buns or sandwich bread. Cover and store in the refrigerator up to 5 days.

GRILLED MARINATED SHRIMP

YIELD: 6 SERVINGS

⅔ cup olive oil
¼ cup chopped fresh parsley
1 lemon, juiced
3 dashes hot pepper sauce
3 garlic cloves, minced
1 teaspoon seasoned salt (purchased, or use recipe
    on pages 26–27)
½ teaspoon ground black pepper
2 pounds large shrimp, peeled and deveined
Vegetable oil
Metal skewers

1. In a medium bowl, combine olive oil, parsley, lemon juice,
   hot sauce, garlic, seasoned salt, and black pepper. Set aside.
   Add shrimp to mixture. Let marinate in the refrigerator for
   about 3 hours.
2. Preheat grill for medium-low heat. Thread shrimp onto the
   metal skewers.
3. Lightly oil grill grate. Cook shrimp directly over heat source
   3–4 minutes per side. Serve hot.

TIP: I like to use metal skewers because wood skewers tend to burn on the grill.

GRILLED FLANK STEAK

YIELD: 8 SERVINGS

This is the cut of beef that's so good in fajitas. And it's also a fantastic entrée on its own.

¾ cup olive oil
⅓ cup red wine vinegar
4½ tablespoons Dijon mustard

4 garlic cloves, minced
2 shallots, chopped
1 tablespoon minced fresh thyme
1 tablespoon minced fresh rosemary
1 tablespoon, plus 1 teaspoon coarsely ground black pepper
2 teaspoons seasoned salt, divided (purchased, or use
   recipe on pages 26–27)
3 flank steaks (about 1¼ pounds each)
Fresh thyme sprigs
Fresh chopped parsley

1. Make marinade: In a medium bowl, whisk the oil, wine vinegar, mustard, garlic, shallots, thyme, rosemary, 1 tablespoon black pepper, and 1 teaspoon salt. Place steaks in large bowl. Pour marinade on steaks, coating each side. Cover and refrigerate overnight.
2. Grill the steak: Prepare grill for medium-high heat. Season steak with remaining teaspoon salt and remaining teaspoon black pepper. Lower heat to medium and grill steaks directly over heat source, covered, until desired doneness. (For medium-rare, a meat thermometer should read 130–140°F; medium, 140–150°F; well-done, 160°F.) Let steak rest 10 minutes. Thinly slice steaks across the grain. Arrange slices on a serving platter and garnish with thyme and fresh parsley.

LEMON GRILLED CHICKEN

YIELD: 4 SERVINGS

4 boneless, skinless chicken breast halves
¾ cup fresh lemon juice
¼ cup olive oil, plus 2 tablespoons
3 garlic cloves, minced
1 teaspoon dried oregano

1 teaspoon chopped fresh parsley
Seasoned salt to taste (purchased, or use recipe
   on pages 26–27)
Ground black pepper to taste

1. Place chicken in a large bowl. Marinade by adding the lemon juice, ¼ cup olive oil, garlic, oregano, parsley, salt, and pepper. Make sure the chicken is covered with the marinade. Store 3–8 hours in the refrigerator.
2. Remove chicken from refrigerator ½ hour before ready to cook.
3. When ready to cook, preheat the grill for medium heat. Brush remaining 2 tablespoons of oil on a sheet of aluminum foil large enough to hold the 4 chicken breasts. Place chicken on foil directly over heat source and grill until done, about 8–10 minutes on each side (depending on the thickness of the chicken). Do not overcook. Serve hot.

GRILLED LAMB CHOPS

YIELD: 6 SERVINGS

¼ cup chopped garlic
¼ cup olive oil, plus 2 tablespoons
½ cup lime juice
Seasoned salt to taste (purchased, or use recipe
   on pages 26–27)
Ground black pepper to taste
3 teaspoons dried parsley
6 lamb chops

1. Make marinade: In a medium bowl, add garlic and ¼ cup olive oil. Marinate the garlic and olive oil at room temperature for 2–4 hours.
2. To this mixture add lime juice, seasoned salt, pepper, and

parsley. Place chops in marinade; cover and refrigerate 4 hours.

3. Grill lamb chops: Preheat the grill for medium heat. Brush each side of chops with remaining 2 tablespoons of oil. Grill until slightly pink on the insides, about 5–8 minutes per side (depending on thickness of the chops). Watch carefully; do not overcook. Serve hot.

GRILLED FRESH CORN SALAD

YIELD: ABOUT 4 SERVINGS

6 ears fresh corn, husked
2 tablespoons corn oil, divided
⅔ cup red bell pepper, diced
⅔ cup diced red onion
¼ cup red wine vinegar
1 tablespoon minced fresh thyme
2 teaspoon minced fresh chives
2 shallots, minced
½ teaspoon salt
¼ teaspoon ground black pepper
½ cup olive oil

1. Prepare a grill for high heat. Blanch corn 8 minutes in enough boiling water to cover corn. Drain well. Rub corn with 1 tablespoon oil.
2. Put oiled corn on hot grill directly over heat source and cook until lightly browned all over. When cool enough to handle, cut kernels off cob and discard cobs.
3. In a small bowl, mix together bell pepper and onion. In a separate large bowl, combine corn, remaining 1 tablespoon oil, bell pepper mixture, red wine vinegar, thyme, chives, shallots, salt, and pepper. Mix well. Gradually add olive oil to salad; toss well. Serve warm.

GRILLED VEGETABLE KABOBS

YIELD: 4 SERVINGS

A few years ago, my older sister from the Tennessee town of Gates made these kabobs at her home. After the vegetables were chopped, she let her grandkids help thread the skewers while she tended the grill. The children had a great time and couldn't wait to do more. This recipe uses bottled dressing and so is easy to assemble. And your kids, too, will love helping out. I think it's important to encourage youngsters to cook. Not only will time in the kitchen help them become well-rounded, but you may just plant the seed for them to become a chef.

When Earl and I were caterers in Milwaukee we always hired teenaged students to help serve food at events. Our young employees were particularly helpful at making sandwiches and putting salads into serving cups. We also taught our helpers how to keep soda dispensers and food areas clean. These tasks were our way of giving teenagers a chance to develop important work skills, in addition to helping them earn money for school.

12 large fresh mushrooms, white button or shiitake
Boiling water
¼ cup bottled Italian dressing
2 tablespoons lemon juice
1½ teaspoons Worcestershire sauce
2 medium zucchini, cut into 2-inch diagonal slices
8 cherry tomatoes
4 metal skewers

1. Prepare a grill to medium heat. Place mushrooms into a medium bowl and add enough boiling water to cover mushrooms. Let stand 1 minute, then drain. Set aside.
2. In a small bowl, combine Italian dressing, lemon juice, and Worcestershire sauce. Thread mushrooms and zucchini alternately onto the skewers.
3. Grill kabobs about 8–10 minutes directly over heat source, turning and brushing frequently with dressing mixture. Remove from heat. Thread 2 cherry tomatoes onto each skewer. Continue grilling 5 minutes, turning and brushing with remaining dressing mixture. Serve hot.

FRESH GRILLED VEGETABLES

YIELD: 4 SERVINGS

2 cups fresh corn cut from cobs
½ cup green pepper, cut into strips
1 cup sliced onion
8 cherry tomatoes, cut in halves
1 tablespoon fresh chopped parsley
¼ teaspoon dried basil
½ teaspoon lemon pepper
½ teaspoon dried thyme
Seasoned salt to taste (purchased, or use
    recipe on pages 26–27)
Ground black pepper to taste
2 teaspoons unsalted butter

1. Prepare a grill on high heat. In a large bowl, combine the corn, green pepper, onion, tomatoes, parsley, basil, lemon pepper, thyme, seasoned salt, and pepper.
2. Place vegetables on enough aluminum foil to hold them and place on grill directly over heat source. Drizzle melted butter over the vegetables. Fold all ends of the foil to seal the vegetables inside.
3. Grill until tender, about 15–20 minutes. After removing from grill, let vegetables sit a few minutes in the foil. Carefully unwrap and remove vegetables to a serving bowl. Serve hot.

OVEN-BAKED BARBECUED MEATBALLS

YIELD: 20 (1-INCH) MEATBALLS

The following two recipes are good for those days you just have to have barbecue, but the weather is not cooperating.

1 pound ground beef or ground chuck
1 cup cracker crumbs

2 eggs, slightly beaten

¼ cup chopped onion

¼ cup whole milk

1 teaspoon seasoned salt (purchased, or use recipe
on pages 26–27)

½ teaspoon ground black pepper

½ teaspoon minced garlic

⅔ cup ketchup

⅓ cup cold water

3 tablespoons brown sugar

1 teaspoon fresh chopped parsley

1. Preheat oven to 350°F. In a large bowl, mix the ground beef, cracker crumbs, eggs, onion, milk, seasoned salt, pepper, and garlic. Form about 20 meatballs; then place in a 9×13–inch casserole dish. In a separate bowl, whisk together the ketchup, water, and brown sugar. Pour mixture over meatballs.
2. Bake until the meatballs are no longer pink in the center, about 40–45 minutes. Place meatballs and any accumulated sauce in a serving bowl; sprinkle with parsley; serve hot.

BARBECUED CHICKEN PIZZA

YIELD: 4 SERVINGS

1 (12-inch) prebaked pizza crust

½ cup barbecue sauce (purchased, or use recipe
on page 82)

2 skinless and boneless chicken breast halves, cooked
and cubed

¼ cup chopped red bell pepper

¼ cup chopped green bell pepper

¼ cup chopped red onion

¼ cup chopped fresh cilantro
½ cup shredded Monterey Jack cheese
½ cup Cheddar cheese
1 teaspoon dried parsley
Olive oil

1. Preheat oven to 400°F. Place pizza crust on a cookie sheet. Spread barbecue sauce evenly over crust.
2. Place chicken over top of sauce. Sprinkle evenly with red pepper, green pepper, onion, and cilantro. Top with Monterey Jack and Cheddar cheeses, and sprinkle with parsley. Lightly drizzle olive oil on top of cheese.
3. Bake until cheese is melted, 12–14 minutes. Serve hot.

SOUTHERN BARBECUE SAUCES BY REGION

The idea of putting sauce on food goes back to when a group of prehistoric chefs discovered that they could improve the flavor of meat with smoke, leaves, and salt. In fact, the word "sauce" is said to come from an ancient word for salt. At some point in time cooks began adding to the flavor profile by basting meat with vinegar, wine, and oils. Sauce took on a new meaning when preserved meats, and especially dried meats, were soaked in liquids to bring them back to life. The resulting dishes could more accurately be defined as stews, which were swimming in sauces made from water, oil, juices, and dairy.

Over the years, daubing barbecue sauce onto meat has become more and more popular, even with purists who claim smoke is all the flavor a piece of meat needs. And in the South, where barbecuing has been raised to an art, the different styles of sauce vary by region, with the five main categories named after their place of origin: Memphis; North Carolina; Kansas City; the Piedmont; and Texas.

Memphis is renowned for pulled pork shoulder doused in a sweet tomato-based sauce (eaten as a sandwich or as an entrée). North Carolina goes big and believes in smoking the whole hog using a ketchup-and vinegar-based sauce, while in the Piedmont area, folks prefer smothering already-cooked and smoked pork with a thin, slightly more vinegary sauce. Kansas City likes their pork cooked with a dry rub. Texans in relative proximity to Tennessee prefer pulled-pork, while just about everywhere else in the Lone Star State you're likely to find beef, especially mesquite-grilled "cowboy-style" brisket. And if it's sauced, the sauce will be made from tomatoes and slightly sweet.

In this section, I have included the five regional styles of barbecue sauce. If you find any of these recipes too spicy for your palate, just reduce or omit the pepper.

MEMPHIS-STYLE BARBECUE SAUCE
YIELD: ABOUT 3 CUPS

Memphis barbecue is renowned for tomato and vinegar-based sauces that occupy the middle ground between the other major styles. Centering around tomatoes, vinegar, brown sugar, and spices, but not too thick, these blends provide moderate amounts of sweet, heat, and tang, with a lot of flavor. In many Memphis restaurants, meat is first rubbed with dry seasoning then smoked over hickory wood without sauce. In this case, the finished barbecue is served with barbecue sauce on the side. As a Tennessean, I grew up enjoying Memphis-style barbecue with the thick sauce clinging to the meat. But there's one case where I do love adding barbecue sauce to cooked meat, and that's on my smoked pork sandwich.

2 tablespoons unsalted butter
¼ cup finely chopped onion
2 tablespoons minced garlic
1 cup ketchup
½ cup water
2 tablespoons molasses
2 tablespoons yellow prepared mustard
2 tablespoons brown sugar
1 tablespoon Worcestershire sauce

1 tablespoon paprika
2 teaspoons mild chili powder
2 teaspoons dried oregano
1 teaspoon salt
½ teaspoon ground black pepper
1 cup apple cider vinegar

1. Melt butter in a saucepan over a medium heat. Add onion and garlic and sauté until lightly browned.
2. Add ketchup, water, molasses, mustard, brown sugar, Worcestershire sauce, paprika, chili powder, oregano, salt, and pepper. Stir in cider vinegar. Reduce heat and simmer over low heat for 20 minutes. Let cool.

TIP: For a smoother sauce, puree in a blender or food processor.

NORTH CAROLINA–STYLE CHICKEN SAUCE
YIELD: ABOUT 2 CUPS

This easy-to-make recipe is based on vinegar and works well with smoked or pulled chicken.

1 cup apple cider vinegar
½ cup ketchup
2 tablespoons brown sugar
2 tablespoons Worcestershire sauce
1 tablespoon unsalted butter
2 teaspoons salt
2 teaspoons hot pepper sauce
½ teaspoon ground black pepper

Combine all ingredients in a small saucepan and simmer 10 minutes. Once chicken is cooked, shred and add sauce to coat.

PIEDMONT PORK BARBECUE SAUCE

YIELD: ABOUT 2½ CUPS

The area known as the Piedmont runs along the Appalachian mountain range from New Jersey south all the way to Alabama. However, this sauce is closely related to what you'll find in North Carolina, and it's based on tomatoes, and is slightly spicy and has the tang of vinegar. This classic barbecue sauce is perfect for pork sandwiches, and it's loaded with flavor.

1½ cups cider vinegar
½ cup ketchup
½ cup water
1 tablespoon white sugar
1 teaspoon salt
¼ teaspoon red pepper flakes
⅛ teaspoon ground black pepper

Mix all ingredients in a quart jar. Cover and refrigerate for several days, allowing the flavors to blend. Shake well before using.

KANSAS CITY–STYLE BARBECUE SAUCE

YIELD: ABOUT 3 CUPS

This tomato-based barbecue sauce is sweet, with a slight touch of molasses, making it similar to what we use in Memphis. The difference is the cayenne, which gives the sauce a little kick. Also, in Kansas City this sauce is mostly doused on beef, as well as pork.

1¼ cups ketchup
1 cup water
⅓ cup cider vinegar
¼ cup dark brown sugar
2 tablespoons molasses

1 tablespoon onion powder
1 tablespoon garlic powder
1 tablespoon ground black pepper
1 teaspoon celery salt
1 teaspoon allspice
1 teaspoon cayenne (optional)

Combine all ingredients in a saucepan and bring to a boil over medium heat. Stir constantly 5 minutes. Reduce heat to low and simmer 20 minutes, stirring occasionally. Sauce should be thick. Allow to cool at room temperature. Store in an airtight container and refrigerate.

TEXAS-STYLE BARBECUE SAUCE

YIELD: 3½ CUPS

Overall, Texas is known for a tomato-based barbecue sauce that's slightly spicy and barely sweet. But regional styles do vary. For example, central Texas was settled by Germans, and there, still, the European practice of heavily smoking pork and beef is popular, and this area's sauces often contain liquid smoke. In east Texas, folks like to barbecue pork shoulder and ribs with a tomato/vinegar-based sauce similar to what's found in Tennessee and Arkansas, and this style can be traced back to newly freed slaves who migrated to Texas.

¼ cup unsalted butter
¼ cup minced onion
3 stalks celery, chopped
1 cup water
1 beef bouillon cube
1 cup ketchup
½ cup cider vinegar
3 tablespoons Worcestershire sauce
2 tablespoons spicy mustard
2 tablespoons honey

2 cloves minced garlic
1 tablespoon paprika
1 tablespoon chili powder
Salt to taste
Ground black pepper to taste

1. Melt butter in a medium sauce pan. Add onion, and celery. Sauté until lightly browned.
2. Add water and bouillon cube. Stir until bullion is dissolved. Stir in ketchup, vinegar, Worcestershire sauce, mustard, honey, garlic, paprika, chili powder, salt, and pepper.
3. Simmer, stirring often, for about 15 minutes. Cool at room temperature and store in the refrigerator.

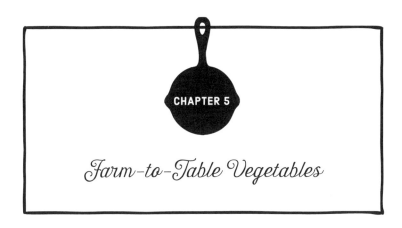

CHAPTER 5

Farm-to-Table Vegetables

GREAT cooking starts with great ingredients, and the best ingredients come from local farms. And it doesn't get any better than walking outside and picking fresh cucumbers or peppers from your own backyard. I know that the greens I pick from my garden taste a lot better than those I purchase at the grocery store; that level of freshness can't be duplicated.

Today, the farm-to-table movement is championed by many in the agriculture, food service, and restaurant communities, as well as by home cooks. That's interesting, since during the early twentieth century, most food that Americans consumed was transported from fewer than 75 miles from their homes. But as country dwellers began moving to the city, many urban food outlets vanished, necessitating that food be brought in from faraway states. To make matters worse, as lifestyles became more hectic, fresh vegetables were often replaced with time-saving processed foods that were quick and easy to prepare but frequently contained excessive amounts of sugar, fat, and sodium.

Modern research shows that if eaten on a regular basis, processed foods can lead to serious health problems, such as high blood pressure, high cholesterol, and heart disease. Thankfully, times certainly are changing, and more people are beginning to realize the importance of eating local, homegrown produce. Even in restaurants, there is a stronger demand for something different and more nutritious. This trend is prompting chefs to embrace farm-to-table ingredients, with much of it purchased locally.

If you don't grow your own garden, don't worry. You still can find the freshest sweet corn, the reddest heirloom tomatoes, and the most flavorful collard greens at farmers' markets and roadside stands. These days, almost every city has at least one farmers' market. Many of these vendors give away samples and will let you taste their heirloom vegetables and hard-to-find foods, such as ramps, morel mushrooms, turnips, cardoons, and quince. I love going to the farmers' market on Saturday mornings, and that's where I always purchase my herb plants and yellow summer squash. And if you have a sweet tooth like I do, you can usually find house-made jams and home-baked breads and pastries.

Back in Halls, my grandmother had one of the largest vegetable gardens in town. And the things she didn't plant, we bought from local farmers, who would come by in their pickup trucks loaded with goodies, such as freshly picked corn on the cob, red, ripe tomatoes, and loosely packed fresh greens. So there were always plenty of fresh vegetables all summer long. Tending a vegetable garden was a popular pastime during those hard times, and even today it's still a great way for families to stretch a budget dollar.

As I still see it, one big advantage of the farm-to-table movement is that the produce I buy at my local farmers' market is not as expensive as store-bought, and I'm always on the side of making a dollar go further. More than being kind to the budget, however, farm-to-table vegetables are fresh and simple, and certainly good for your health. Consuming local produce also takes us back to our roots, to the time when we once valued quality over convenience. And as a bonus, when you buy local, you support small farmers.

SPINACH AND STRAWBERRY SALAD

YIELD: ABOUT 4 SERVINGS

1 bunch baby spinach, rinsed
12 large strawberries, hulled and sliced
½ cup white sugar

⅓ cup white wine vinegar
½ teaspoon salt
½ teaspoon ground black pepper
1 cup vegetable oil
¼ cup pecan pieces

1. In a large bowl, mix the spinach and strawberries. Set aside.
2. In a food processor, combine the sugar, white wine vinegar, salt, black pepper, and oil. Blend until smooth. Stir in the pecans. Pour over the spinach and strawberries. Toss to coat. Serve immediately.

GARDEN-FRESH BLT SALAD

YIELD: 8–10 SERVINGS

This recipe is best made with the freshest tomatoes, lettuce, baby spinach, cucumber, basil, and green onions you can find. This is certainly a healthy salad, and it's a wonderful summer recipe to make when your garden is brimming with ripe vegetables.

1 head lettuce, torn into bite-sized pieces
3 large tomatoes, thinly sliced
½ cup diced celery
5 hard-boiled eggs, sliced
½ cup diced green pepper
1 cup diced onion
8 slices bacon, cooked and crumbled
1 recipe Easy Dressing for BLT Salad (recipe follows)
⅔ cup grated cheese, any kind
Chopped green onion for garnish

1. In a large dish, layer lettuce, tomatoes, celery, eggs, green bell pepper, onion, and bacon. Spread dressing over salad.
2. Sprinkle with grated cheese and green onions. Serve immediately.

EASY DRESSING FOR BLT SALAD

YIELD: 2½ CUPS

Sometimes I just don't have the time to make salad dressing from scratch, and this adaptation works just fine. And when I do use bottled dressing, I make sure to buy a brand that doesn't have artificial ingredients.

2½ cups bottled ranch salad dressing
1½ tablespoons white sugar

Mix salad dressing and sugar together. Refrigerate until ready to use.

BROCCOLI AND RAISIN SALAD

YIELD: ABOUT 4–6 SERVINGS

This salad can be made even more healthful by substituting turkey bacon for regular bacon. Your family will love this one.

2 cups fresh broccoli florets
1 cup chopped red onion
1 recipe Sour Cream Salad Dressing
    (recipe follows)
½ cup golden raisins
8 bacon strips, cooked and crumbled, or ¼ cup cooked
    turkey bacon

Break broccoli into small, bite-sized pieces. In a medium bowl, toss broccoli with onion. Pour dressing over broccoli and onion mixture. Scatter raisins and bacon over vegetables. Refrigerate until ready to serve. Serve cold.

SOUR CREAM SALAD DRESSING

YIELD: 1½ CUPS

1 cup mayonnaise
½ cup sour cream
1 tablespoon vinegar
1 teaspoon white sugar
2 dashes Worcestershire sauce

Blend all ingredients together. Can be made 2 days ahead and stored, covered, in the refrigerator.

FRESH GARDEN PASTA SALAD

YIELD: 8–10 SERVINGS

The combination of pasta and fresh crunchy garden vegetables is absolutely irresistible, and I make this often. For a complete meal you can add 1 cup chopped, cooked chicken or 2 cups fresh, cooked shrimp. Children enjoy making this recipe.

1 (12-ounce) package uncooked tricolor spiral pasta
Salt for cooking pasta
2 stalks celery, chopped
2 cups diced fresh red tomatoes
½ cup thinly sliced carrots
½ cup chopped green bell pepper
½ cup chopped onion, red or white
½ cup peeled and thinly sliced cucumber
2 (16-ounce) bottles Italian-style salad dressing, preferably
    without artificial ingredients
½ cup grated Parmesan cheese

1. In a large pot, cook pasta according to package directions. Rinse under cold water; drain. Set aside.
2. In a large bowl, add celery, tomatoes, carrots, bell pepper, onion, and cucumber. Mix well.
3. Combine cooled pasta with vegetables. Pour Italian dressing over mixture and mix well. Add Parmesan cheese and mix well. Chill at least 1 hour before serving.

SPAGHETTI AND CUCUMBER SALAD

YIELD: ABOUT 6–8 SERVINGS

This dish goes well with just about any meat entrée. I included a similar recipe in my second cookbook and have since discovered that this salad is great alongside chicken wings and meatballs; it is also a tasty addition to any party menu. And I'll bet you won't find this cold spaghetti dish served on many tables. So if you're looking for something deliciously different, try this recipe. For a complete one-dish meal, add cooked meatballs, cooked shrimp, or crabmeat, and serve with dinner rolls.

6 ounces spaghetti, uncooked
Seasoned salt to taste (purchased, or use recipe
   on pages 26–27)
Ground black pepper to taste
Garlic powder
5–6 ounces Basil Pesto Spread, or more to taste (purchased,
   or use recipe on pages 84–85)
3 medium red tomatoes, chopped
2 cucumbers, peeled and chopped

1. Cook spaghetti according to package directions and drain. Cool by running cold water over spaghetti in a colander. Drain well.
2. In a large bowl, season spaghetti with seasoned salt, black pepper, and garlic powder. Add pesto spread and mix well.

3. One hour before serving, add tomatoes and cucumbers. Mix well. Taste, and if more pesto spread is needed, add ½ teaspoon at a time.

FRIED GREEN TOMATOES

YIELD: 4–6 SERVINGS

When I was growing up, Big Mama would fry green tomatoes she picked fresh from her garden. Today still, I feel that if you're going to fry green tomatoes, it's best to pick them directly from the garden; the flavor and texture are just superior. Another secret is to soak the slices in buttermilk so that the coating sticks better.

Although there are varieties of tomatoes that are green when ripe, the green tomato to use for frying is any type of tomato that is not yet ripe. Ripe tomatoes, even green varieties, turn mushy when battered and fried.

This recipe, like so many others in this book, has been in my family for generations, and it's a recipe that, until now, was never written down; it was just something we all knew how to cook. That said, fried green tomatoes is certainly a southern staple, and it has inspired many to create websites, songs, books, and even the movie Fried Green Tomatoes. *This dish is great served with your favorite entrée.*

> 3 medium green tomatoes
> 1 cup buttermilk
> Seasoned salt to taste (purchased, or use recipe on pages 26–27)
> Ground black pepper to taste
> ⅛ teaspoon ground red pepper (optional)
> 1 cup cornmeal
> ⅓ cup all-purpose flour
> Vegetable oil for frying

1. Slice tomatoes into ⅓-inch slices. In a small bowl, add buttermilk; then add the tomatoes. Let tomatoes marinate in

buttermilk 20 minutes. Remove tomatoes from mixture and lightly shake off excess.

2. Season tomatoes well on each side with seasoned salt, black pepper, and red pepper. In a separate bowl, mix the cornmeal and flour. Batter both sides of each tomato slice in the cornmeal mixture.

3. Pour oil into a large heavy pot or skillet to a depth of 1½ inches and heat on medium heat. Fry tomatoes on each side until golden brown. Drain on a paper towel. Serve hot.

TURNIP GREENS WITH SMOKED MEAT

YIELD: 8–10 SERVINGS

Southerners love their greens, and there's nothing more comforting than a well-seasoned pot of fresh turnip greens. Turnips grow in the fall and winter. The plant's green tops are smaller and more tender than collards. The turnip plant is scientifically known as Brassica rapa, *and it belongs to the Cruciferae family. It is also a cousin to other health-protective cruciferous vegetables, such as kale, cabbage, and broccoli. The slightly bitter bite of turnip greens is actually delicious. For the best taste, pick greens in the fall in the morning, after the dew has fallen.*

Turnips greens were always a favorite vegetable in our family. Early in the morning, my grandmother would go to her garden and pick "a mess of greens," an old term that my family used to use. In addition to eating greens, I enjoy turnip greens cooked with the turnip root (see recipe for Garden-Fresh Turnip Roots on pages 108–109). I like mine topped with chopped onions and red, juicy, sliced tomatoes, and I always dip into the savory potlikker with a big piece of Big Mama's Hot-Water Corn Bread (recipe on pages 129–30).

3 ounces smoked meat (salt pork, also known as
    boiling meat, or ham hock)
2 quarts water
1 cup chopped onion, divided
1 teaspoon red pepper flakes

4 pounds fresh turnip greens
2 tablespoons bacon fat (vegetable oil will also work)
2 tablespoons white vinegar
Salt and ground black pepper to taste

1. Place pork in a large pot. Add water, ½ cup onion, and pepper flakes. Cover and bring to a boil. Reduce heat and continue cooking on medium heat until meat is tender. (If you use a ham hock, this will take at least 2–3 hours.) Remove from heat, but do not drain. Prepare turnip greens for cooking, (see instructions below).
2. Add half of greens to pot with smoked meat, along with bacon fat, vinegar, remaining ½ cup onion, salt, and pepper. Let greens cook down and add remainder. Cover and continue cooking for 35–40 minutes, or until greens are tender. Serve greens in individual bowls, along with pot-likker (vegetable's cooking juice).

PREPARING TURNIP GREENS FOR COOKING
Wash greens:

1. Fill a sink halfway with cool water and add greens, being sure they are completely submerged.
2. Using both hands, dip a few leaves at a time in and out of the water. Remove cleaned leaves to a colander.
3. Repeat process for 2–3 washings or until all dirt and grit are removed.

Prepare greens for cooking:

1. Start from the pointed top of the greens, fold a leaf in half lengthwise and remove the stem by tearing the leaf away from the stem and discarding stem. Turnip greens leaves are tender so they don't need to be cut into bite-size pieces.
2. Repeat process until all greens are prepared.

TIP: In the South, turnip greens are usually easy to find in backyard vegetable gardens, on farms, and in farmers' markets.

GARDEN-FRESH TURNIP ROOTS

YIELD: ABOUT 4 SERVINGS

During the antebellum period, the turnip was considered a poor-quality vegetable, so it became known as a food fit only for African slaves. As time went on, slave owners learned that a pot of turnip greens made with ham bones or whatever meat was around tasted pretty good, and today the lowly turnip is a signature dish for southerners of all stripes.

Turnips are actually enjoyed by both rich and poor around the world. However, in the United States turnips are not plentiful in grocery stores as are other root vegetables, such as beets and carrots. If you have a hard time finding them, you can certainly grow your own or scout them out at farmers' markets. And increasingly they are gracing the menus of upscale southern-style and soul food restaurants. I like my turnip roots mixed in a pot of fresh turnip greens, and I always finish that off with Southern Skillet Corn Bread (recipe on pages 128–29).

> 3 cups fresh turnip roots, peeled and quartered
> ¼ cup white sugar
> 3 tablespoons unsalted butter
> Seasoned salt to taste (purchased, use recipe on pages 26–27)
> Ground black pepper to taste
> ½ teaspoon red pepper flakes
> Water or vegetable stock (purchased, or use recipe
>   on pages 67–68)
> 2 tablespoons fresh chopped parsley

1. In a medium pot, add turnips, sugar, butter, seasoned salt, black pepper, red pepper flakes, and enough stock to cover turnips halfway. Turn heat to medium and bring to a boil.

Cover and cook until turnips are fork-tender, about 15–20 minutes.

2. Sprinkle with fresh parsley and serve hot, or mix with cooked turnip greens.

MASHED TURNIPS WITH POTATOES

YIELD: 6 SERVINGS

2 cups peeled and cubed turnip roots
2 cups peeled and cubed white potatoes
Water
¼ cup whole milk
2 cloves garlic, minced
3 tablespoons unsalted butter, divided
1 teaspoon white sugar
1 teaspoon seasoned salt (purchased, or use recipe on pages 26–27)
¼ teaspoon ground black pepper
½ teaspoon red pepper flakes (optional)
1 teaspoon dried parsley

1. Preheat oven to 375°F. Grease a 9 × 13–inch baking dish.
2. In a large pot over medium heat, cover turnips and potatoes with water. Bring to a boil and cook until tender, about 20 minutes. Remove from heat; drain.
3. To pot of cooked turnips, add milk, garlic, 2 tablespoons butter, and sugar. Season with seasoned salt, black pepper, and red pepper flakes. Mash turnips and potatoes; mixture should still be lumpy.
4. Transfer mixture to prepared baking dish. Top with bits of remaining 1 tablespoon butter and dried parsley. Cover and bake 15 minutes. Remove cover and continue to bake until lightly browned, about 10 more minutes. Serve hot.

SOUTHERN FRIED OKRA

YIELD: 4–6 SERVINGS

Studies show that okra originated around Ethiopia and was cultivated by the ancient Egyptians by the twelfth century BC. The vegetable then spread throughout North Africa and the Middle East, where seed pods were often cooked, toasted, and ground up and used as a coffee substitute. This alternative for coffee is still used today. In the 1700s, okra came to the Caribbean and the United States with the West African slave trade, and it was introduced to western Europe shortly after.

Unless it's cooked properly, the natural mucilage in okra can turn slimy. Even so, we southerners love our okra, and we find it excellent fried or sautéed. It's also fat-free, low in calories, and a good source of vitamins C and A.

Okra is a tropical member of the mallow family, and it grows rapidly in warm temperatures, with the plant's edible, elongated seed pods usually ready in 60 days. This vegetable is popular worldwide, and it is consumed in Africa, the Middle East, Greece, Turkey, India, the Caribbean, South America, as well as the southern United States.

1 cup vegetable oil
20 fresh okra pods, 3–5 inches long
Cold water
1½ cups cornmeal
2 tablespoons all-purpose flour
1 teaspoon salt
½ teaspoon ground black pepper

1. Heat oil in a skillet over medium heat. Cut okra into ⅓-inch slices. Wash in cold water and set aside.
2. In a small bowl, mix cornmeal, flour, salt, and black pepper. Dredge okra in cornmeal mix and fry until golden brown, about 3–5 minutes. Drain on paper towels. Serve immediately.

BAKED YELLOW SQUASH

YIELD: 8 SERVINGS

I always make this recipe with locally grown summer squash, and it is best served with anything barbecued, grilled, or smoked.

3 pounds yellow summer squash, cut into 1-inch cubes
Water
¾ cup dry bread crumbs, divided
½ cup chopped onion
2 eggs
¼ cup melted unsalted butter, plus ⅓ cup, divided
1 tablespoon white sugar
1 teaspoon salt
1 teaspoon parsley
½ teaspoon ground black pepper
½ teaspoon garlic powder
½ teaspoon red pepper flakes (optional)

1. Preheat oven to 350°F. Grease a 9×13–inch casserole dish and set aside.
2. Add squash to a large pot and add just enough water cover. Boil until soft, about 15–20 minutes. Drain squash until all liquid is removed. Place in a large bowl and mash slightly. Squash should still be chunky.
3. Add ½ cup of bread crumbs, onion, eggs, ¼ cup of butter, sugar, salt, parsley, black pepper, garlic powder, and red pepper flakes. Mix until completely combined, and transfer mixture to prepared baking dish. Drizzle remaining ⅓ cup melted butter on top of casserole. Sprinkle remaining bread crumbs over the butter.
4. Bake until the casserole top is golden-brown, about 45 minutes to 1 hour. Serve hot.

BUTTERED SKILLET SQUASH

YIELD: 4–6 SERVINGS

The last time I made this recipe, I purchased the squash from the farmers' market where I live, and the completed dish disappeared really fast. That squash was so delicious we ate it by the bowlful; I've always loved hot buttered squash.

½ cup unsalted butter, softened
6 medium yellow squash, cut into ¼-inch slices
1 cup chopped onion
1 tablespoon white sugar
⅓ cup water
Seasoned salt to taste (purchased, or use recipe
   on pages 26–27)
Ground black pepper to taste
½ teaspoon red pepper flakes (optional)
Garlic powder to taste
Fresh chopped parsley

1. Heat butter in a large skillet over medium heat. Add squash, onion, sugar, water, salt, pepper, red pepper flakes, and garlic powder. Cover and cook, stirring occasionally, until a darker shade of yellow but still firm, 10–15 minutes. Add more water if needed.
2. When done, the butter and water should have absorbed slightly into the squash. Sprinkle fresh parsley on top and serve hot.

FRIED CABBAGE SKILLET

YIELD: ABOUT 4–6 SERVINGS

This recipe is a quick way to serve a fresh vegetable in no time, and I often make it when I'm in a hurry. I feel it's ideal served with meat loaf (recipe on page 30) or macaroni, cheese, and sausage casserole (recipe on pages 21–22).

3 tablespoons vegetable oil
5 cups green cabbage, cut into bite-sized pieces
½ cup chopped onion
1 tablespoon red or white vinegar
½ teaspoon ground red pepper (optional)
Seasoned salt to taste (purchased, or use recipe
    on pages 26–27)
Ground black pepper to taste

In a large skillet over medium-low heat, add oil. Let it get hot and add cabbage, onions, vinegar, red pepper, seasoned salt, and black pepper. Stir and cook until cabbage is fork-tender, about 10–12 minutes. If cabbage starts to stick, add about ½ cup water. Serve hot.

TWICE-BAKED SWEET POTATOES

YIELD: ABOUT 4 SERVINGS

This recipe is a sweet alternative to the traditional twice-baked white potato and to the holiday sweet potato casserole everyone seems to serve. Sweet potatoes are not only good, they're extremely healthful. This root vegetable is available year-round and is rich in potassium and fiber. It contains no fat or cholesterol, and without butter or oil has about 105 calories.

4 medium sweet potatoes
½ cup (1 stick) unsalted butter, softened
½ cup brown sugar
3 tablespoons white sugar
⅔ cup evaporated milk
2 tablespoons ground cinnamon, divided
1 tablespoon ground nutmeg
20 miniature marshmallows

1. Preheat oven to 375°F. Wash and dry potatoes. With a fork,

make 3–4 pricks in potato skins. On a baking pan, bake potatoes until tender, 50–60 minutes.

2. In a bowl, mix butter, brown sugar, white sugar, and milk.
   Add cinnamon and nutmeg. Set aside.

3. Once potatoes are done, remove from oven and let cool
   until they can be handled. Cut potatoes lengthwise and
   scoop out pulp; put in a medium bowl. Add the butter
   mixture to the potatoes and mix well. Take a taste, and if it
   needs to be sweeter, add more white sugar.

4. Stuff each potato skin with the sweet potato mixture. Top
   each sweet potato half with about 5 marshmallows. Lightly
   sprinkle with cinnamon. Return stuffed sweet potatoes to
   oven and bake until hot and the marshmallows have melted,
   about 10 minutes.

FRIED SWEET POTATOES

YIELD: 4–6 SERVINGS

*I call this recipe "sweet potato pie in a skillet" because the taste reminds me
of an old-fashioned sweet potato pie. I found this recipe in my great-grand-
mother's recipe collection. I also found a note written by my great-grand-
mother on the recipe saying that she would always serve these potatoes with
homemade chicken and dumplings (recipe on pages 16–17). That's how her
mother served this dish, too. Well, I will certainly keep the tradition going. I
guess some things never change.*

4 medium sweet potatoes
½ cup (1 stick) unsalted butter, softened
2 cups white sugar
2 tablespoons cinnamon
1 teaspoon freshly grated nutmeg
½ cup water, more if needed
1 teaspoon vanilla extract

Peel and cut potatoes lengthwise into ¼-inch pieces. In a

cast-iron skillet over medium heat, mix together potatoes, butter, sugar, cinnamon, nutmeg, water, and vanilla. Cover and cook until the potatoes are fork-tender and the sugar turns into a light syrup, about 30 minutes. If needed, add more water ¼ cup at a time. Serve hot.

FRIED COB CORN

YIELD: ABOUT 8–10 SERVINGS

Nothing hits the spot like a fresh bowl of hot buttered corn. My dad used to make fried corn often for my mom, who worked second shift at the Tupperware Company in Halls, and who would love coming home to a skillet of fresh fried corn.

I remember my father pulling up a stool to the kitchen stove when he was beginning to prepare this dish. Typically, he had just purchased the corn from a local farmer who drove through the neighborhood with a truckload of corn on the cob fresh from the field. If you bought a dozen ears, the farmer would give you another dozen at no cost; that's just the way he was. And if there were neighbors who wanted corn but didn't quite have enough money, he would just give them a brown paper bag full. Just seeing that generous gentleman drive down Cedar Street in his old pickup truck was a real treat because we knew we would soon be eating Dad's fried corn.

My dad would make his fried corn when I was dating my husband, and today, still, Earl talks about that delicious fried corn. I re-created this recipe from my memory of my dad's special dish.

10–12 ears fresh, sweet yellow corn
2 tablespoons all-purpose flour
1 tablespoon white sugar
1 cup (2 sticks) unsalted butter, softened, divided
Salt to taste
Ground black pepper to taste
½ cup bacon fat
Water

1. Cut corn from cob. Scrape a few cobs to get the juice, and

add it to corn mixture. (If kernels are large, make several cuts into the kernels before scraping, and this will help cook evenly.)

2. In a medium bowl, combine the corn, flour, sugar, ½ cup butter, salt, and black pepper. Mix well.

3. Heat bacon fat in a very large skillet or Dutch oven over medium-low heat and let it get hot. Add corn mixture and ½ cup water to hot skillet. Add remaining ½ cup butter and stir. Reduce to low heat; stir frequently for 5 minutes. Add water as needed to keep corn from sticking.

4. Adjust for salt and pepper, and if you don't have much cob juice, add ½ cup water. Cover and cook at a bare simmer until corn is done and almost all moisture is absorbed, about 45 minutes, stirring occasionally. The corn kernels should still be whole and not mushy. Remove from heat and allow to sit, covered, 5 minutes. Stir well and scrape up any bits that may have accumulated at the bottom. Serve hot.

TIP: Don't be afraid to add all the butter and lots of salt and pepper; the corn should be well-seasoned.

ROASTED RED POTATOES

YIELD: 6–8 SERVINGS

The potato is the world's fourth-largest food crop, following rice, wheat, and maize, and was first cultivated by the Inca in Peru around 8,000 BC to 5,000 BC. The average American consumes about 142 pounds of potatoes every year. Whether you roast, bake, or fry this comfort food, potatoes are the number-one vegetable crop in the world. They're available year-round because they are harvested somewhere every month of the year.

12–14 mini-sized red potatoes
¼ cup olive oil
¼ cup unsalted butter, melted

1 teaspoon seasoned salt (purchased, or use recipe
    on pages 26–27)
1 teaspoon black pepper
1 teaspoon garlic powder
1 teaspoon dried basil
½ teaspoon dried thyme

1. Preheat oven to 425°F. Peel a half strip of potato peel, starting from the center to the end of each potato. Place potatoes
   on an ungreased baking sheet. In a large bowl, combine
   oil, butter, seasoned salt, pepper, garlic powder, basil, and
   thyme. Drizzle mixture over each potato, making sure all
   sides are coated.
2. Bake uncovered until potatoes are fork-tender, 25–35
   minutes.

TIP: Purchase mini-sized potatoes that are all basically the same size so the
potatoes will roast evenly.

SOUTHERN POTATO SALAD
YIELD: 6–8 SERVINGS

*This flavor-packed potato salad is my family's old summer favorite for picnics
and weekend barbecues. It's also a great way to incorporate fresh vegetables into
meals.*

5 cups white potatoes, peeled and cut into cubes
Water
2 tablespoons white vinegar
Seasoned salt to taste (purchased, or use recipe
    on pages 26–27)
Ground black pepper to taste
1 tablespoon white sugar
1 tablespoon yellow prepared mustard

1–1½ cups mayonnaise or salad dressing
1 cup sweet pickle relish, or more to taste
½ cup chopped celery
½ cup chopped white or red onion
2 green onions, chopped
½ cup chopped green bell pepper
3 hard-boiled eggs, peeled and chopped
1 cup chopped red tomatoes
2 teaspoons fresh chopped parsley
Paprika

1. In a medium pot, cover potatoes with water and boil, covered, until potatoes are fork-tender but still firm. Drain well. Make sure all liquid is removed.
2. In a large bowl, combine potatoes, vinegar, seasoned salt, pepper, sugar, mustard, mayonnaise, and relish. Blend well.
3. Add celery, white or red onion, green onion, green bell pepper, boiled eggs, tomatoes, and parsley. Mix gently. Taste, and add more relish if needed. Sprinkle with paprika. Keep cold until time to serve.

OVEN-BAKED POTATO CASSEROLE
YIELD: ABOUT 6–8 SERVINGS

This baked potato casserole is something the whole family will enjoy. It's also a great way to get rid of those extra potatoes hanging around the kitchen.

For the past several years, baked potatoes have been gaining popularity and are now served at many fast-food restaurants as a side order. This dish gets its creaminess and a punch of flavor from sour cream and the evaporated milk. Oh, and don't forget about the crispy bacon on top, a delicious touch. This recipe will most definitely be a winner on your dining table.

3 pounds white potatoes, peeled and cut into 1-inch pieces
Water

⅔ cup evaporated milk

½ cup sour cream

3 tablespoons unsalted butter

2 cloves garlic, minced

Seasoned salt to taste (purchased, or use recipe
   on pages 26–27)

Ground black pepper to taste

1 tablespoon fresh chopped parsley, divided

2 cups shredded Cheddar cheese, divided

8 slices bacon, cooked and crumbled, divided

1. Preheat oven to 350°F. Grease a 9 × 13–inch casserole dish.
2. Add potatoes to a large pot and cover with water. Cook, covered, over medium heat until tender, 15–20 minutes. Drain and return potatoes to pot.
3. Add evaporated milk, sour cream, butter, garlic, seasoned salt, pepper, and half the parsley. Mix until smooth. Stir in 1½ cups cheese and half the bacon. Mix well and pour mixture into prepared casserole dish.
4. Bake until heated all the way through, 20–25 minutes. Top with remaining ½ cup cheese, remaining bacon, and remaining parsley. Bake until cheese is melted, another 4–5 minutes. Serve hot.

SOUR CREAM CUCUMBERS

YIELD: 4–6 SERVINGS

2 fresh cucumbers, peeled and thinly sliced

1 small red onion, thinly sliced

⅓ cup sour cream, regular or low-fat

2 tablespoons chopped fresh dill

1 tablespoon white vinegar

1 tablespoon water

1 teaspoon minced garlic

½ teaspoon seasoned salt (purchased or use recipe
   on pages 26–27)
¼ teaspoon ground black pepper
¼ teaspoon ground red pepper (optional)
Fresh parsley sprigs

1. In a medium bowl, add cucumbers with red onion slices. Set
   aside.
2. In a separate bowl, mix together sour cream, dill, vinegar,
   water, garlic, seasoned salt, black pepper, and red pepper.
   Add to cucumber mixture. Mix to coat. Chill and garnish
   with fresh parsley.

HEALTHY AND LIGHT COLESLAW
YIELD: 6–8 SERVINGS

This healthy coleslaw is certainly a winner on any table.

4 cups finely shredded green cabbage
2 cups finely shredded red cabbage
¾ cup shredded carrots
⅓ cup chopped green or red onion
⅓ cup low-fat mayonnaise
¼ cup low-fat plain yogurt
2 tablespoons white vinegar
1 teaspoon white sugar
Seasoned salt to taste (purchased, or use recipe
   on pages 26–27)
Ground black pepper to taste

1. In a large bowl, combine green and red cabbages, carrots,
   and onion. Set aside.
2. In a separate bowl, combine mayonnaise, yogurt, vinegar,
   sugar, seasoned salt, and pepper; blend well. Add mayon-

naise mixture to cabbage; mix together. Cover and chill before serving.

FRIED RED ONION RINGS

YIELD: 4 SERVINGS

Compared to yellow onions, red onions have a slightly sweet, yet pungent flavor. They have no fat or cholesterol, and a ½-cup serving contains only about 32 calories. The fiber in red onions helps improve the functioning of the digestive tract, and they're loaded with vitamins and minerals.

Red onions are often enjoyed raw in salads or sliced on sandwiches. And even though conventional wisdom says to only serve them uncooked, I use them as a main seasoning in hot dishes, such as turnip greens, pinto beans, and peas. Red onions are also a great addition to any vegetable garden.

Vegetable oil for frying
1 cup buttermilk
2 medium red onions, cut into ⅓-inch slices and
　separated into rings
1 cup all-purpose flour
2 teaspoons seasoned salt (purchased, or use recipe
　on pages 26–27)
1 teaspoon ground black pepper
½ teaspoon garlic powder
⅛ teaspoon dried rosemary
½ teaspoon cayenne pepper (optional)

1. In a large skillet, heat oil to 375°F. In a medium bowl, add buttermilk and soak onion rings in buttermilk 15 minutes. Remove rings from buttermilk. Set aside.
2. In a medium bowl, add flour, salt, pepper, garlic powder, rosemary, and cayenne. Mix well. Dip onion rings in flour mixture.
3. Fry rings in hot oil until golden brown, about 1–2 minutes on each side. Serve immediately.

FARM CROWDER PEAS

YIELD: ABOUT 6 SERVINGS

The crowder pea is a variety of the species commonly called "cowpeas" or "southern peas" and is related to black-eyed peas and field peas. Actually a bean, the brown, roundish crowder came to the New World from Africa in the 1600s.

Crowder peas are rich in fiber and potassium, and they contain good amounts of calcium, magnesium, and phosphorus. I used to help my grandmother pick crowder peas from her garden, and like so many southerners, we would put the peas in bags and freeze them for the winter months.

I love crowder peas served with sliced onions, and I usually cook them at least twice a month.

> 3 ounces smoked meat (or boiling meat or
>   ham hock)
> 5 cups water
> ½ cup chopped onion, divided
> 3 cups crowder peas, fresh or frozen
> 2 tablespoons bacon fat or vegetable oil
> 2 tablespoons white vinegar
> ½ teaspoon red pepper flakes (optional)
> Seasoned salt to taste (purchased, or use recipe
>   on pages 26–27)
> Ground black pepper to taste
> 2 dashes of red hot sauce (optional)

1. In a medium pot, add meat, water, and half the onion. Cover and cook over medium heat until meat is just tender. (If using ham hock, this will take 2–3 hours.)
2. Add peas, bacon fat, vinegar, remaining onion, red pepper flakes, seasoned salt, and pepper. Cook over high heat until peas start to boil. Reduce heat to medium-low and continue cooking, covered, until peas are tender, about 20–25 minutes.

3. Add hot sauce about 10 minutes before peas are done. The red pepper sauce does not make the peas spicy; it just adds flavor. When done, peas should be firm but not mushy. Serve hot.

BRUSSELS SPROUTS AND POTATO STIR-FRY
YIELD: ABOUT 8 SERVINGS

With this recipe, you have the best of farm-to-table-fresh Brussels sprouts, fresh potatoes, and colorful red and green bell peppers.

1 tablespoon olive oil
1 cup chopped onion
1 cup white potato, peeled and cubed
1 pound fresh Brussel sprouts, halved, ends trimmed and
    yellow leaves removed
1 cup fresh chopped red bell pepper
½ cup fresh chopped green bell pepper
½ cup chicken broth or stock (purchased, or
    use recipe on pages 65–66)
1 teaspoon kosher salt
½ teaspoon freshly ground black pepper
Fresh chopped parsley

1. In a large skillet over medium heat, heat the olive oil. Add onion and potato. Cook and stir until the onion is transparent, about 3–5 minutes.
2. Add Brussels sprouts, red bell pepper, green bell pepper, and chicken broth. Cover and cook until vegetables are tender, about 10–12 minutes.
3. Toss with salt and black pepper. Garnish with fresh parsley. Serve hot.

SKILLET GREEN BEANS AND POTATOES

YIELD: 6–8 SERVINGS

Green beans with red potatoes ranks pretty high on my list of favorite things to eat. In fact, my grandmother planted green beans, and my older sister and I would help her snap them for dinner. This is a simple vegetable to make and doesn't really take long to put together. My grandmother often made green beans with red potatoes and served it with Southern Skillet Corn Bread (recipe on pages 128–29). What a delicious combination.

6 slices bacon, chopped, or 3 ounces of ham
3 tablespoons unsalted butter
½ cup chopped white onion
2 pounds fresh green beans, trimmed and snapped
2 cups diced red potatoes, washed and unpeeled
¼ cup chicken broth or stock (purchased, or use recipe on pages 65–66)
2 teaspoons white vinegar
½ teaspoon red pepper flakes (optional)
Seasoned salt to taste (purchased, or use recipe on pages 26–27)
Ground black pepper to taste
Fresh chopped parsley

1. In a large skillet over medium heat, add the bacon and cook evenly until browned, 8–10 minutes. Drain well on a paper towel. Set aside.
2. In another large skillet over medium heat, melt the butter. Stir in the onion and cook until translucent, about 5 minutes. To the onion mixture, add cooked bacon, green beans, potatoes, chicken broth, vinegar, red pepper flakes, seasoned salt, and black pepper. Bring to a boil. Cover and cook over low heat until the green beans and potatoes are tender, about 15–20 minutes. Green beans and potatoes should still be firm. Sprinkle with fresh parsley. Serve hot.

Southern Sweet Tea
(pages 206–207)

Mama's Sunday Pot Roast with Brown Onion Gravy
(pages 33–35)

Parslied Mayonnaise Drop Rolls

(page 142)

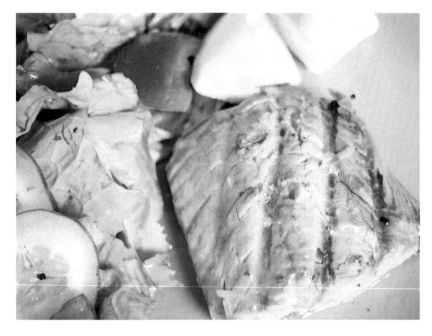

Easy Grilled Salmon
(pages 82–83)

Bacon and Mushroom Soup
(pages 53–54)

Chicken and Corn Bread Dressing with Giblet Gravy
(pages 17–20)

Buttered Skillet Squash
(page 112)

Earl's Pinto Bean Soup with Big Mama's Hot-Water Corn Bread
(pages 51–52, 129–30)

Coconut Cake with Creamy Coconut Frosting
(pages 155–56)

Strawberry Butter Roll with Strawberry Sauce
(pages 191–92)

Mama's Egg Custard Pie
(pages 199–200)

Elnora's Sweet Milk and Jelly Cake
(pages 159–60)

Southern Pecan Bars
(pages 179–80)

Peach Ice Cream

(pages 194–95)

CHAPTER 6

King Corn Bread and
Other Traditional Southern Breads

Let's face it, no proper southern meal is complete without a big piece of homemade corn bread. Sure, we love soft white rolls, slices of whole wheat bread, and, of course, biscuits. But no bread compares in popularity to the "meal finisher," corn bread, the backbone of southern cooking and that wonderful sponge for soaking up all our tasty sauces and potlikker juices.

Why so much talk about corn bread? Native Americans introduced corn to European settlers, who immediately made the grain a staple food. And even though corn has always grown in both southern and northern states, corn became the preferred grain crop of the humid South, where wheat often refused to grow.

During the nineteenth century, stone-grinding corn mills that produced-whole-grain meal were extremely popular, and they offered the only way for many farm families to get any kind of meal. In the early twentieth century, many mills changed from stone to steel grinding. That's when most of the hull and germ started being removed. That's also when the moisture content of cornmeal became lower, and when cooks first started putting sugar in corn bread to make up for the dry texture. Today, few home cooks have access to corn mills, and the cornmeal we use is typically fine-grained and prepackaged, and it makes outstanding corn bread. But if you look hard enough, you can find stone-ground cornmeal—meal that retains some of the hull and germ—and then you can make corn bread as it was meant to be.

I suppose one reason we natives of Halls, Tennessee, remain connected to corn bread throughout our lives is that many young mothers transition their toddlers from baby food to solid food by feeding the youngsters mashed pieces of corn bread soaked in potlikker. The women in my family certainly keep up this "first food" tradition. And that combination of corn bread and the savory juices from well-seasoned greens makes me hungry just thinking about it. Even today, at my age, I can't imagine eating greens without hot-water corn bread.

Although we like to claim it as our own, corn bread is enjoyed throughout the United States, and there are many regional differences in its preparation. In the Southwest, cooks often use blue cornmeal. Northern regions favor using yellow cornmeal, while the South prefers white cornmeal. Probably the biggest regional difference in corn bread is the addition of sugar. On the whole, southern corn bread is usually made with little or no sugar, and therefore does tend to be less sweet. Southern corn bread recipes also call for less flour, and are traditionally made with white cornmeal and buttermilk. Northern corn bread is much sweeter, has more flour, and has more of a cakelike texture and feel. When it comes to corn bread, I'm not picky. I'll eat it either way, with or without sugar. In fact, one time I tasted corn bread made by a home cook in Wisconsin, and I thought I was eating pound cake—but it was extremely delicious.

Even though my family is naturally drawn to corn bread, we do love quick breads made with baking powder, and, of course, hot, fluffy biscuits. The biscuit as we know it originated in southern plantation kitchens. Back then, before the invention of baking powder, beaten biscuits—biscuits made light by exhaustively beating the dough—were especially common.

The base recipes for traditional southern breads date back centuries, and many are still made today, including those for biscuits and muffins, along with corn-based southern skillet corn bread, hoecakes, hot-water corn bread, crackling bread, and southern corn pone. Each is slightly different, has a unique characteristic, and is packed with flavor.

A FEW TRADITIONAL SOUTHERN CORN BREADS

- Southern Skillet Corn Bread—A cornmeal and buttermilk base that's baked in the oven until golden brown.
- Hot-Water Corn Bread—Bread fried on top of the stove and made with cornmeal, egg, and hot water instead of milk.
- Hoecakes—A fried bread similar to hot-water corn bread, but made without eggs.
- Crackling Bread—Similar to hot-water corn bread with pieces of pork crackling added. Can be fried or baked.
- Hush Puppies—Fried and seasoned balls of corn bread batter.
- Spoonbread—An oven-baked bread made with milk, egg, and butter. Very moist and should be served with a spoon.
- Southern Corn Pone—One of the earliest corn breads. A simple cornmeal batter of water and salt originally cooked in a cast-iron skillet or Dutch oven directly over hot coals.

A FEW OF OUR FAVORITE BREADS MADE WITH WHEAT FLOUR

- Biscuits—This all-American favorite is made with flour, baking soda, and buttermilk and baked in the oven until golden brown.
- Muffins—A quick bread cooked in small, round cups, giving the finished bread a deep round shape.
- Quick Breads—Wheat dough leavened with baking powder and/or baking soda and cooked in the shape of a loaf.

COOKING CORN BREAD WITH A CAST-IRON SKILLET

Ask any southerner, and they'll tell you that baking corn bread in a heavy iron skillet is the only way to get that golden-brown top, that crusty texture around the edges, and the perfect moist interior.

Before being used, any new cast-iron skillet must go through a process called seasoning. To season a skillet properly, oil is baked into the skillet's surface, and that provides a protective seal that will usually last a lifetime and will prevent bread or any other food from sticking. It's sort of like when you season your food, it tastes better. Well, when you season a skillet, it performs better. And I'm all for anything that will make my life a little easier in the kitchen. Here are five easy steps to help you season your own skillet.

EASY STEPS TO SEASON A CAST-IRON SKILLET

1. Preheat the oven to 350°F. Do not use the oven to bake food during this process.
2. Wash the skillet with soap and completely scour it with a scrub brush. Dry the skillet well.
3. Use a paper towel to completely coat the inside and outside with lard, vegetable shortening, or olive oil, making sure every inch is covered.
4. Place the skillet in the oven for two hours. During this time, the oil will penetrate the skillet. Remove the skillet from the oven and allow it to cool.
5. Beginning with step number 3, repeat this process two more times. This assures that you have a good nonstick surface that won't strip off when you cook food. From then on, do not clean your skillet with a metal scrubber or you will scrape off the coating and have to season it all over again.

SOUTHERN SKILLET CORN BREAD
YIELD: 6 SERVINGS

For years, there has been a hot debate over whether corn bread should include sugar. I believe this depends on how you were taught, and I disagree with cooks who think sugar has no business in corn bread. I do feel sugar helps develop corn bread's flavors, and it makes the texture moister. And if a little sugar will get the kids to eat bread, it's worth a try. So if your family enjoys corn bread made with sugar, by all means, add it. You be the one to decide.

¼ cup bacon fat or vegetable oil
2 cups self-rising white cornmeal

½ cup all-purpose flour

1 egg

1 cup buttermilk or whole milk

1 tablespoon white sugar (optional)

1. Preheat oven to 375°F. Pour bacon fat into a 9-inch cast-iron skillet and heat in oven 5 minutes.
2. In a medium bowl, mix together cornmeal, flour, egg, buttermilk, and sugar. Blend well.
3. Pour about ¼ of hot oil from skillet into the batter and mix slightly. Pour batter into hot skillet and bake until golden brown, about 20–25 minutes. Serve warm.

BIG MAMA'S HOT-WATER CORN BREAD

YIELD: 8–10 BREAD PATTIES

My grandmother taught me how to make hot-water corn bread. As a young girl, I would stand up in a chair in the kitchen and watch the process. After Big Mama mixed all the ingredients together in a bowl, she would drop a spoonful of batter into hot oil in a thick, black skillet on top of the stove. And I was so small at the time, I really didn't realize what was going on. My mother always baked her corn bread in the oven, and I never really understood why Big Mama's corn bread technique was so different.

When I got older, I learned that hot-water corn bread is made with hot water instead of milk, and that it's fried like small pancakes in vegetable oil on top of the stove. This was the very first bread I ever made, and today it's my favorite bread to make. I was about twelve years old the first time I made it, and it came out all right. But over the years, and through lots of trial and error, I learned to perfect my recipe.

One of Big Mama's tips was to make sure the water is very hot, not luke-warm. She also added a little sugar to her bread, so I add a little sugar to mine. The sugar is optional, and the amount in the recipe won't sweeten the bread; it only slightly changes the texture by making it more tender.

My husband, too, is a big fan of hot-water corn bread, and he doesn't want his bread fixed any other way. And I like this recipe because frying the bread instead of baking it saves valuable time in the kitchen.

> Fresh vegetable oil
> 2 cups self-rising white or yellow cornmeal
> 2 tablespoons all-purpose flour
> 1 large egg
> 1 tablespoon white sugar (optional)
> 1½ cups extremely hot water

1. Heat ½ inch of vegetable oil over medium heat in a large cast-iron skillet until oil is hot but not smoking. In a large bowl, combine cornmeal, flour, egg, and sugar. Stir in hot water a little at a time until batter is slightly thicker than a pancake batter.
2. For each bread patty, drop 1 serving spoon (3 tablespoons) of cornmeal batter into skillet. An average skillet will hold about 4–5 patties at oné time.
3. Fry until small bubbles start to form around the edges; then turn on the other side. Slightly press on the center of the patty so that it will cook evenly inside. The patties are done when the outsides are golden on both sides, after 3–5 minutes of total cooking. They should be crisp on the outside and moist on the inside. Cool patties slightly on paper towels and serve.

FRIED CRACKLING BREAD

YIELD: 6 SERVINGS

Cracklings are pieces of pork or fat trimmings sliced into bite-sized pieces and fried until brown and crispy. These little hard balls of fat are delicious when added to corn bread and biscuit recipes. They're also fantastic scrambled with eggs, and many cooks use cracklings to season vegetable dishes such as cabbage, greens, beans, and peas, and in gravies and sauces. Growing up, crackling bread was a real treat. On special occasions, sometimes Big Mama would put about a half cup of cracklings in her hot-water corn bread batter.

Cracklings are not only popular in the South. In Poland, pork cracklings are known as skwarki. *In Croatia and Serbia, pork cracklings are called* čvarci. *In Yiddish, chicken cracklings are known as* gribenes.

½ cup bacon fat or vegetable oil
2 cups self-rising white or yellow cornmeal
2 tablespoons all-purpose flour
1 large egg
½ cup cracklings (grated in a food processor, or
    purchased pre-grated)
1 tablespoon white sugar (optional)
1½ cups hot water

1. Heat oil in a large cast-iron skillet over medium heat until hot but not smoking.
2. In a large bowl, combine cornmeal, flour, egg, cracklings, sugar, and hot water. Mix well. For each bread patty, pour 1 serving spoon (3 tablespoons) of cornmeal mixture into hot skillet. An average skillet will hold about 4–5 patties at one time.
3. Fry in hot oil until small bubbles start to form around the edges; then turn on the other side. To assure that the insides cook evenly, slightly press on the center of each patty. Cook until golden on both sides, about 3–5 minutes total. Cool patties on paper towels.

OVEN CRACKLING BREAD

YIELD: 6 SERVINGS

This recipe uses cracklings in traditional whole milk corn bread that's baked in the oven.

¼ cup vegetable oil
1½ cups self-rising cornmeal
½ cup all-purpose flour

1 large egg, beaten

1½ cups whole milk or buttermilk

½ cup cracklings (purchased already grated, or
   grate in a food processor)

1. Preheat oven to 375°F. Heat oil in an 8-inch cast-iron skillet
   in the oven until hot but not smoking.
2. In a medium bowl, sift together cornmeal and flour. Stir in
   egg, whole milk, and cracklings. Mix well and pour batter
   into hot greased pan. Bake in oven until golden-brown,
   about 20–25 minutes. Do not overbake. Serve warm.

TRADITIONAL SOUTHERN SPOONBREAD
YIELD: SERVES ABOUT 12

*Spoonbread is a puffy baked bread made with egg, butter, and sugar, and its
sweet, buttery corn flavor reminds me of a light cornmeal soufflé. Unlike
firm-textured regular corn bread, spoonbread is best eaten with a spoon. It makes
a fantastic side dish and is a good replacement for rice and potatoes. Spoonbread
is also a natural side to salty breakfast foods, such as ham, bacon, and sausage.
Just remember to enjoy it with a spoon!*

*Although some historians believe this special dish probably originated after the
Civil War, many say that spoonbread can be traced back to the Native American
porridge called* suppone *or* suppawn. *Sarah Rutledge, author of the cookbook*
The Carolina Housewife *(1847), researched spoonbread history back to Native
Americans.*

½ cup (1 stick) unsalted butter, plus 1 tablespoon

4 cups whole milk

1 cup yellow cornmeal

4 eggs, lightly beaten

2 tablespoons white sugar

1 tablespoon baking powder

¾ teaspoon salt

1. Preheat oven to 375°F. Butter the inside of an 8 × 8–inch baking pan or a 1½-quart casserole dish with 1 tablespoon butter. Set aside.
2. In a large saucepan over medium-high heat, add milk and remaining ½ cup butter. When the milk boils, whisk in cornmeal and cook until thoroughly mixed. Remove from heat and allow to cool. Set aside. As mixture starts to cool, it will get slightly get thick.
3. In a medium bowl, add eggs, sugar, baking powder, and salt. Pour into cornmeal mixture and mix well. Transfer to prepared casserole dish.
4. Bake until golden brown on top, about 30–40 minutes. Serve hot.

HOECAKES

YIELD: ABOUT 12

There are conflicting stories about where the hoecake got its name. Hoecakes were a staple with African slaves, who liked to eat the simple corn flatbread with molasses. Many food historians claim the hoecake was invented on plantations by these slaves, who baked the bread on the blade of a hoe over open fires. Others say the hoecake was created by Native Americans, who ground corn into meal, kneaded the meal into dough, and baked their cakes on an open fire. Regardless of who first made them, these cornmeal pancakes are inextricably tied to the cuisine of the American South.

Hoecakes are often made without egg or milk, similar to hot-water corn bread. And since they call for few ingredients, they're extremely budget-friendly. This recipe is simple to make, even if you don't have a hoe and an open fire.

½ cup bacon fat or vegetable oil
2 cups yellow or white cornmeal
1 teaspoon salt
2 cups hot water

1. Heat bacon fat in a large skillet over medium heat.
2. In a large mixing bowl, blend the cornmeal, salt, and hot water. Mix well.
3. For each bread patty, place about 1 heaping tablespoon of cornmeal mixture into hot skillet. An average skillet usually holds about 4 patties at one time. Fry until small bubbles start to form around the edges. Turn on the other side and slightly press on the center of the patty to ensure that the inside cooks evenly. Cook until golden on both sides, for a total of 3–5 minutes. Drain on paper towels and serve warm.

OLD-FASHIONED DRESSING BREAD
YIELD: 6–8 SERVINGS

I use this recipe to make the corn bread for my homemade Chicken and Corn Bread Dressing (see pages 17–19). Because it's made to be used in dressing, the texture is chunkier than that of traditional corn bread. But the combination of fresh vegetables and poultry and sage seasonings makes it extremely flavorful, and it is great served with greens, beans, peas, or any dish you would normally eat with corn bread.

⅓ cup vegetable oil
1 cup self-rising white cornmeal
2 tablespoons all-purpose flour
1½ cups whole milk
1 large egg, slightly beaten
½ cup finely chopped white onion
½ cup finely chopped celery
½ cup finely chopped green pepper
1 tablespoon poultry seasoning
2 teaspoons rubbed sage

1. Preheat oven to 375°F. Heat oil in a 9-inch cast-iron skillet or a 9×13–inch baking dish in the oven until oil is hot but not smoking.

2. While oil is heating, in a large bowl, mix the cornmeal, flour, milk, egg, onion, celery, and green pepper. Mix well. Add poultry seasoning and sage. Mix well. Pour mixture in hot baking dish with oil and bake until the top is golden brown, about 20–30 minutes. Serve hot with butter, or allow to cool for use in the recipe for Chicken and Corn Bread Dressing (pages 17–19).

CHEESY SKILLET CORN BREAD
YIELD: 6 SERVINGS

Is there any better way to dress up corn bread than with bacon, jalapeño peppers, and pepper jack cheese? And this one is gluten-free, to boot.

4 pieces thick-sliced bacon
2 fresh jalapeño peppers, minced
1 cup yellow cornmeal
1 cup whole milk
¾ cup gluten-free flour
2 tablespoons white sugar
1 tablespoon baking powder
½ teaspoon salt
½ teaspoon dried parsley
2 eggs
¼ cup unsalted butter, melted
1 cup shredded pepper jack cheese, divided
2 green onions, chopped

1. Preheat oven to 425°F. In a 9-inch cast-iron skillet over medium-high heat, cook bacon until brown and crisp, about 10 minutes. Leave bacon fat in the skillet and drain the bacon slices on paper towels. When cool enough to handle, crumble bacon into small pieces. Set aside.
2. In reserved bacon fat, cook jalapeño peppers until lightly browned. Set aside.

3. In a medium bowl, combine cornmeal and milk. Let this sit until some of the liquid absorbed, about 5 minutes.

4. In a separate bowl, combine flour, sugar, baking powder, salt, and parsley. Add the eggs and butter into cornmeal mixture and stir until moist. Thoroughly mix the flour mixture into the cornmeal mixture. Add ½ cup pepper jack cheese and green onions. Pour batter into the skillet with the jalapeño peppers. Sprinkle crumbled bacon over top, then sprinkle remaining ½ cup cheese over bacon.

5. Bake until set and a toothpick inserted in the center comes out clean, about 20 minutes. Serve warm.

SPICY HUSH PUPPIES

YIELD: 24

Hush puppies are small, deep-fried balls of cornmeal batter seasoned with a little sugar and finely chopped onions. They're traditionally served with cat-fish and coleslaw—at least that's how I like to eat mine. Today, you can find hush puppies in restaurants from North to South. However, this "soul food" is particularly enjoyed by southerners, no matter if they're black or white.

The Ursuline nuns in New Orleans are believed to have created this fried dump-ling in the early 1700s. But there are several tales about the origin of the name "hush puppy." They all have the same basic premise, that either an African cook in Atlanta, a group of southern hunters, or a Creole cook in New Orleans tossed a piece of the fried cornmeal to a howling dog and commanded, "Hush, puppy!"

1½ cups self-rising cornmeal
½ cup sifted all-purpose flour
2 teaspoons white sugar
1 small onion, finely chopped
1 egg, beaten
¾ cup whole milk or buttermilk
1 teaspoon finely chopped jalapeño pepper (optional)
Vegetable oil for frying

1. In a medium bowl, sift together cornmeal, flour, and sugar. Add onion, egg, milk, and jalapeño pepper. Mix well.
2. Heat 2 inches oil over medium heat in a deep skillet or deep-fryer until oil reaches 350°F. For each hush puppy, drop a teaspoon of batter into hot oil. Do not crowd the skillet. Fry several at a time until golden brown, about 2–3 minutes. Drain on paper towels and serve hot.

TRADITIONAL CORN FRITTERS
YIELD: 1 DOZEN

Corn fritters are made with a mixture of corn kernels, eggs, and milk and are usually fried up and served with jam, fruit, or honey. Although corn fritters originated in the South, many cultures have developed similar dishes. For example, Asians eat pakoras, a popular snack made with vegetables dipped in batter and deep-fried using a technique similar to the one used for corn fritters. But nothing takes the place of the traditional corn fritter. This popular southern favorite continues to receive rave reviews, and it even has an entire day named after it: National Corn Fritter Day, held every year on July 16.

Vegetable oil for frying
1 cup sifted all-purpose flour
1 teaspoon baking powder
½ teaspoon salt
½ teaspoon ground black pepper
½ teaspoon white sugar
1 egg, lightly beaten
½ cup whole milk
1 tablespoon vegetable shortening, preferably nonhydrogenated, or butter, melted
1 (12-ounce) can whole kernel corn, drained

1. Heat 1 inch oil in a heavy pot or deep fryer to 350°F.
2. In a medium bowl, combine flour, baking powder, salt,

pepper, and sugar. Mix well. Add egg, milk, and shortening, and stir into flour mixture. Add the corn kernels. Mix well.

3. Scoop batter with a cookie scoop or a ¼-cup measuring cup, and drop into the hot oil. Fry until golden-brown on all sides, about 2–3 minutes. Drain on paper towels. Serve immediately.

CREAMED CORN FRITTERS

YIELD: ABOUT 12–14 FRITTERS

Turn these fritters into something special by serving with sorghum, molasses, or maple syrup.

Vegetable oil for frying
1 cup of self-rising flour
½ teaspoon white sugar
Salt to taste
Ground black pepper to taste
1 tablespoon butter, melted
1 teaspoon minced onion
1 teaspoon garlic powder
1 teaspoon minced fresh parsley (optional)
1 egg, beaten
2 dashes red pepper sauce
½ of a (15-ounce) can of creamed corn

1. Heat 1 inch oil in a fryer to 325°F. In a large bowl, blend together flour, sugar, salt, black pepper, butter, onion, garlic powder, and parsley. Mix well. Stir in egg, red pepper sauce, and creamed corn. Mix well.

2. Scoop batter with a cookie scoop or a ¼-cup measuring cup and drop into the hot oil. Fry until golden-brown on all sides, about 2–3 minutes. Drain on paper towels. Serve immediately.

SOUTHERN CORN PONE

YIELD: 2 DOZEN SMALL CAKES

Authentic southern corn pone is a simple cake made without milk or eggs and typically fried on top of the stove and served with butter and sweet spreads.

½ cup bacon fat or vegetable oil
4 cups yellow cornmeal
1 tablespoon salt
2–3 cups hot water

1. Heat bacon fat over medium heat in a large cast-iron skillet on top of the stove.
2. In a medium bowl, mix the cornmeal, salt, and water. Cover batter and let sit 20 minutes to thicken. If batter starts to dry out, add more water.
3. Scoop up batter with a ¼-cup measuring cup. Flatten and shape into a small oval cake. To test if it's ready to cook, press a few fingers across the top of the batter. The batter should feel smooth. Remove your fingers, and if the indentations remain in the dough, the batter is perfect. If not, add more water or cornmeal, whichever is needed.
4. Form the remaining batter into small cakes, and go ahead and put those finger indentations on top of them all; that's a traditional touch. Fry in hot bacon fat until golden brown, about 3 minutes. Turn and brown on the other side, about 3 more minutes. Drain on paper towels and serve warm.

CORN BREAD MUFFINS

YIELD: 12 MUFFINS

¼ cup vegetable oil
1 cup self-rising cornmeal
¾ cup all-purpose flour

1 tablespoon white sugar (optional)
Pinch of salt
1 cup buttermilk
1 large egg, slightly beaten

1. Heat oven to 425°F. Generously grease bottom and sides
   of 12 medium muffin pans with vegetable oil, or line with
   paper baking cups.
2. In a medium bowl, combine cornmeal, flour, sugar, and salt.
   Stir in buttermilk and egg. Mix well.
3. If pan is coated with oil, place pan in oven 5 minutes to get
   oil hot. Fill hot cups about ⅔ full. Bake until tops of muffins
   are slightly golden-brown, about 12–18 minutes. Remove
   immediately from pan. Serve hot.

HERBED CORNMEAL BISCUITS

YIELD: ABOUT 8 BISCUITS

1 cup all-purpose flour
½ cup white cornmeal
1 tablespoon white sugar
1 teaspoon dried thyme
1 teaspoon dried parsley
2 teaspoons baking powder
½ teaspoon salt
½ teaspoon ground black pepper
4 tablespoons cold butter, cut into small pieces
½ cup cold buttermilk

1. Preheat oven to 450°F. In a medium bowl, combine flour, cornmeal, sugar, thyme, parsley, baking powder, salt, and pepper.
2. Add butter to flour mixture and mix with a pastry blender
   or your fingers until mixture is the size of coarse crumbs.
   Add buttermilk and stir until moist.

3. Transfer dough onto a lightly floured board. Form dough into a 4 × 8–inch rectangle. Cut dough with a 2-inch biscuit cutter, or use a sharp knife and cut into 2-inch squares. Place biscuits on an ungreased baking sheet. Bake until golden brown, about 12–15 minutes. Serve hot with Sweet Butter Spread (recipe on page 147).

HOMEMADE BUTTERMILK BISCUITS

YIELD: 6–8 LARGE BISCUITS

I remember my Big Mama getting up on Sunday mornings and making a hearty breakfast before church. Biscuits were always on the menu, and they were usually served with scrambled eggs, fried bacon, and her homemade strawberry jam. My older sister, Debra, and I couldn't wait for Sunday mornings, just so we could enjoy Big Mama's biscuits.

2 cups all-purpose flour
1 tablespoon baking powder
1 tablespoon white sugar (optional)
1 teaspoon salt
¼ cup cold vegetable shortening, preferably nonhydrogenated
½ teaspoon baking soda
1 cup cold buttermilk
Sweet Butter Spread (recipe on page 147)

1. Heat oven to 425°F. In a medium bowl, sift together flour, baking powder, sugar, and salt. Add shortening, baking soda, and buttermilk. Mix well.
2. Transfer dough onto a floured board. Roll out to a thickness of ¼–⅜ of an inch, and cut with a round biscuit cutter or a sharp knife.
3. Bake on an ungreased baking sheet until lightly brown around edges, about 15 minutes. Serve hot with Sweet Butter Spread.

PARSLIED MAYONNAISE DROP ROLLS

YIELD: 1 DOZEN

Unless you're from the South, you may have never heard of mayonnaise drop rolls. Many years ago it was common to add mayonnaise to bread and cake recipes because mayonnaise was an economical substitute for milk and butter, and because it also makes food moist. The mayonnaise in this recipe is not at all noticeable. It only helps makes the rolls light and fluffy.

One Sunday, I made a large batch of these rolls for dinner, and not only did they get rave reviews, but after they got cold, they didn't get hard. The next morning, I heated the leftover rolls for breakfast, and they were still soft, and I served them with butter and strawberry preserves. The next day, the flavors had really developed, and I served my few remaining rolls with Sweet Butter Spread (recipe on page 147).

> 1 tablespoon unsalted butter, softened
> 2 cups self-rising flour
> 1 cup whole milk
> 2 teaspoons white sugar
> 6 tablespoons good-quality mayonnaise
> 2 teaspoons minced fresh parsley, or 1 teaspoon dried

1. Preheat oven to 400°F. Lightly grease a baking sheet with the butter.
2. In a large bowl, stir together flour, milk, sugar, mayonnaise, and parsley. Blend slightly. Drop by tablespoonsful onto baking sheet.
3. Bake in preheated oven until golden-brown, about 20–25 minutes. Serve hot with butter.

SWEET POTATO BISCUITS

YIELD: ABOUT 1½ DOZEN

¾ cup whole milk
1 cup boiled and mashed sweet potatoes
5 tablespoons unsalted butter

1½ cups all-purpose flour
3 tablespoons white sugar
4 teaspoons baking powder
1 teaspoon ground cinnamon
1 teaspoon freshly grated nutmeg
½ teaspoon ground ginger
½ teaspoon salt
Pinch baking soda

1. Heat oven to 425°F. In a large mixing bowl, combine the milk, potatoes, and butter. Add flour, sugar, baking powder, cinnamon, nutmeg, ginger, salt, and baking soda. Blend well.
2. Turn mixture onto a floured board and knead 30–45 seconds. Roll dough about ½-inch thick and cut with a biscuit cutter. Bake biscuits on an ungreased baking sheet until golden brown, about 12–15 minutes. Serve hot.

BROWN SUGAR AND CINNAMON MUFFINS

YIELD: 12 MUFFINS

1½ cups all-purpose flour
¼ cup white sugar
¼ cup brown sugar, packed
2 teaspoons baking powder
1 teaspoon ground cinnamon
1 teaspoon freshly grated nutmeg
1 egg, slightly beaten
½ cup vegetable oil
½ cup whole milk
⅔ cup chopped pecans

1. Preheat oven to 400°F. Grease the bottoms and sides of the cups of a muffin pan, or line with paper baking liners.
2. In a medium bowl, sift together the flour, white sugar, brown sugar, baking powder, cinnamon, and nutmeg. Set aside.

3. In a separate bowl, mix together the egg, vegetable oil, and milk. Add milk mixture to the dry mixture, stirring enough to just moisten all ingredients.
4. Stir pecans into batter. Fill muffin cups ⅔ full. Bake until golden brown, about 15–20 minutes. Serve warm.

TIP: This is a really good breakfast recipe.

SWEET POTATO BREAD

YIELD: 1 (9 × 5–INCH) LOAF

1 cup white sugar
½ cup light brown sugar
½ cup vegetable oil
2 eggs, slightly beaten
1¾ cups all-purpose flour, sifted
1 teaspoon baking soda
½ teaspoon ground cinnamon
½ teaspoon ground nutmeg
½ teaspoon ground ginger
¼ teaspoon salt
½ cup water
1 cup cooked and mashed sweet potatoes
½ cup applesauce

1. Preheat oven to 350°F. Grease a 9 × 5–inch loaf pan.
2. In a large bowl, combine white sugar, brown sugar, and oil. Beat well. Add eggs and mix well. Set aside.
3. In a separate bowl, combine flour, baking soda, cinnamon, nutmeg, ginger, and salt. Stir flour mixture into egg mixture alternately with water. Stir in sweet potatoes and applesauce; mix well.
4. Pour batter into prepared loaf pan and bake until the center springs back when lightly touched, about one hour.

TIP: This moist bread is great served with Sweet Butter Spread (recipe on page 147). And before you start making the batter, make sure the dates on all cooking spices have not expired.

STRAWBERRY PECAN BREAD

YIELD: 2 LOAVES

It's a widely known fact that we southerners love strawberry cobbler, but we also like strawberries in just about anything else, including in breads. This quick bread is a delicious breakfast treat, and it pairs well with salty meats, such as ham, bacon, or sausage.

3 cups all-purpose flour
1 teaspoon salt
2 cups white sugar
1 teaspoon baking soda
1 teaspoon ground cinnamon
1 teaspoon freshly grated nutmeg
1 cup solid vegetable shortening, preferably
　nonhydrogenated
4 eggs, slightly beaten
2 cups sliced fresh strawberries
½ cup chopped pecans

1. Heat oven to 350°F. Grease 2 (9×5×3–inch) loaf pans.
2. In a medium bowl, combine flour, salt, sugar, baking soda, cinnamon, and nutmeg. Use a large spoon to mix in shortening. Add eggs, strawberries, and pecans. Stir until all ingredients are moistened.
3. Spoon batter into prepared pans. Bake until a toothpick comes out clean, about 60–70 minutes. Cool in pans 10 minutes.
4. Transfer loaves to a baking rack to cool completely.

TIP: Leftovers can be wrapped and stored at least four days in the refrigerator. This bread is also great served with Sweet Butter Spread (recipe on page 147).

SPICED PECAN BREAD

½ cup vegetable oil, plus additional for oiling pan
1 cup white sugar
2 eggs
¼ cup sour cream
1 teaspoon vanilla extract
2 cups flour
1 teaspoon salt
1 teaspoon baking soda
¼ teaspoon baking powder
¼ teaspoon ground cinnamon
¼ teaspoon freshly grated nutmeg
⅔ cup chopped pecans

1. Preheat oven to 350°F. Grease and flour a 9 × 5–inch loaf pan. In a medium bowl, combine ½ cup vegetable oil and sugar. Beat well. Add eggs, one at a time, beating after each addition. Stir in sour cream and vanilla. Set aside.
2. In a separate bowl, combine flour, salt, baking soda, baking powder, cinnamon, and nutmeg. Add to egg mixture and beat until well blended. Stir in pecans.
3. Pour into prepared pan and bake until a toothpick inserted in center comes out clean, about 1 hour. Do not overbake. Remove from oven and let cool in pan 10 minutes. Turn out onto a wire baking rack to cool completely.

STRAWBERRY SAUCE

YIELD: ABOUT 3–3½ CUPS

This fresh-tasting sauce is great served on hoecakes, spoonbread, and corn bread.

3 cups white sugar
1 cup water

3 cups fresh strawberries, capped and chopped
2 teaspoons allspice
2 teaspoons freshly grated nutmeg
1 tablespoon freshly squeezed lemon juice

1. In a saucepan, bring sugar and water to a boil over medium heat. Gradually add strawberries. Return to a boil and cook 10 minutes.
2. Reduce heat and add allspice, nutmeg, and lemon juice. Bring to a boil and simmer, uncovered and stirring occasionally, until the mixture thickens, about 25–30 minutes. Serve warm.

TIP: This sauce can be kept in the refrigerator up to seven days. Slightly reheat before serving.

SWEET BUTTER SPREAD
YIELD: ¾ CUP

½ cup (1 stick) unsalted butter, softened
⅓ cup light brown sugar
3 tablespoons honey
½ teaspoon ground cinnamon
½ teaspoon ground nutmeg
¼ teaspoon ground ginger

Combine all ingredients in a medium bowl. Spread butter over hot corn bread, toast, pancakes, and muffins. Can be kept tightly covered in the refrigerator up to one month.

BANANA NUT WHOLE WHEAT LOAF
YIELD: 10–12 SERVINGS

2 cups whole wheat flour
2 tablespoons wheat germ

1 teaspoon iodized salt

1 teaspoon baking soda

1 teaspoon ground cinnamon

¼ cup vegetable oil

½ cup honey

2 large eggs, slightly beaten

2 teaspoons vanilla extract

2 cups mashed bananas

⅔ cup chopped pecans

1. Grease a 9×5–inch loaf pan. Preheat oven to 350°F.
2. In a large bowl, blend together flour, wheat germ, salt, baking soda, and cinnamon. Set aside.
3. In a medium bowl, combine oil, honey, eggs, vanilla, and mashed bananas.
4. Make a well in the center of the dry ingredients. Pour the banana mixture into the dry ingredients. Use a spoon to combine, just until dry ingredients are dampened. Stir in pecans; mix. Pour batter into prepared pan.
5. Bake until a toothpick inserted in center comes out clean, about 1 hour. Cool in pan 10 minutes. Remove from pan and cool completely on a wire rack. Keeps up to 3 days, covered, at room temperature.

CHAPTER 7

Country Cakes

I remember Big Mama putting together her favorite pound cake and the wonderful aromas that filled our house as it baked. But before it went into the oven, she would beat the batter 300 strokes by hand because at that time she didn't own a mixer. She always said that beating the batter by hand makes the batter come out smoother anyway, and, believe it or not, it did.

The word "cake" can be traced back to England in the thirteenth century, the time when cakes were mostly bread-like. And since sugar in this era was expensive and often not available, most cakes were sweetened with honey. Back then it was also common to put dried fruits, nuts, and seeds in cakes. And many medieval European bakers often made fruitcakes and gingerbread because the spices acted as a preservative and cakes baked with them would last several months. Icing during this period was made from sugar, egg whites, and flavorings. It wasn't until the nineteenth century that cakes began to take a different, more familiar form—they were made with refined white flour and baking powder. This was also the time when buttercream frosting started replacing boiled icings. I love buttercream frosting, and I feel that it was a great day for home cooks when this style of cake icing was created.

But what exactly are country cakes? They're anything from the homeliest coconut, lemon, pound, and chocolate cakes to the fanciest hummingbird, carrot, and red velvet cakes we grew up with, and they're all made from scratch using recipes and cooking techniques handed down from one generation to the next. These recipes will never go out of style. And the success of these cakes does not depend only on the recipe; it also revolves around how the recipe is prepared and executed. Before the time of cake mixes, home cooks added their own special touches, "a pinch of this" and a "dash of that" to make a cake their very own. I know because my grandmother, mother, and other family members left me several recipes, along with cooking techniques that make our cakes unique.

The origin of a true country cake is the southern United States. And whenever we need to bake a cake for a church picnic or a gathering of family or friends, we naturally turn to our dog-eared recipes. A particular cake's association with a rural social event is probably where the "country" came from. Regardless, most of us grew up enjoying country cakes, and the recipes for them are priceless and should be put away for safekeeping.

One intangible is that country cakes are made by home cooks with a passion and great love for baking. My mother was an excellent baker, and she put a lot of love into her cakes, especially during the holidays. She would make sure that whatever sweet she baked always came out right, and her country cakes, in particular, were enjoyed by the entire family year after year.

Most country cakes have another thing in common—they're flavored with vanilla. As we all know, vanilla is the most loved of all culinary extracts, and, aside from its use in cake, it adds a pronounced, sensual scent and flavor to many desserts, such as pies, pudding, and cobblers, as well as beverages. I feel that there's nothing you could possibly add to your cake that would take the place of vanilla. Does anything smell better than that amazing aroma, especially when it goes from the bottle into the fresh cake batter? It smells just like perfume. It's also interesting that vanilla, something we now take for granted, is so exotic. Food history shows that long before Columbus arrived in America, the Totonac people in the mountains of Mexico were using vanilla, and that later they started cultivating this member of the orchid family. What a delicious idea.

So whenever I want to bake a country cake, as I dig out my bottle of vanilla and plug in my electric mixer, I always think that what's especially wonderful about these old recipes is that they create extraordinary memories. And that makes them even more valuable. A while back I misplaced my mother's famous Holiday Jam Cake recipe, and I didn't rest until I found it. (The recipe is on pages 161–62.) This was one of her traditional holiday cakes, so not only do I cherish it, but it's part of my treasured collection and very much a part of my history.

DO YOUR CAKE-BAKING SKILLS MEASURE UP?

Do you have good cake-baking skills? All great home cooks know that a great cake is only as good as its ingredients, and that the use of proper technique is crucial. I have a few tips I want to share with you before baking country cakes:

1. Using fresh ingredients is important. If you're making a cake from scratch, check the expiration dates on your ingredients. Big Mama also knew the importance of using fresh ingredients, and she always shopped the day before she did her baking.

2. Be sure to measure and sift dry ingredients. This helps to eliminate even the smallest lumps that may not be visible. Sifting also combines dry ingredients uniformly, and that results in a better-textured cake. When Big Mama would put together her pound cake, I used to watch her sift the ingredients through a metal sifter.

3. Cleanliness is another key element in successful baking. Make sure supplies such as bowls, mixing beaters, spoons, measuring cups, and baking pans have been properly washed before using. Also make sure the area used for baking is clean and free of clutter.

4. Measuring ingredients correctly is an important part of the cake-baking process.

5. A big mistake some bakers make is not choosing the correct measuring tools. For accurate measuring, always use indi-

vidual measuring cups instead of multipurpose measuring cups, especially for dry ingredients. Individual cups allow you to level off excess ingredients and help you to measure more accurately. Also, preset measuring spoons are better than regular kitchen spoons. Again, it's easier to level off measuring spoons. Baking pans are also important in this process. They should be in good condition, and you should use the size pan that the recipe specifies. Using the wrong-size pan will cause the cake to turn out less than perfect.

6. Remember, whether you're baking a cake for a special event or for a family meal, baking is an enjoyable experience for the cook, and the sight of a country cake is a good way to bring smiles to many faces.

BEST CARROT CAKE

YIELD: 10–12 SERVINGS

1½ cups vegetable oil
2 cups white sugar
3 large eggs
2 teaspoon ground cinnamon
2 teaspoons vanilla extract
2 teaspoons baking soda
1 teaspoon salt
½ teaspoon freshly grated nutmeg
2 cups grated raw carrots
2 cups all-purpose flour
½ cup crushed pineapple, with liquid
½ cup chopped pecans
Cream Cheese Frosting for Best Carrot
    Cake (recipe follows)

1. Preheat oven to 350°F. Grease and flour a 9 × 13–inch pan or glass baking dish.

2. In a large bowl, combine oil, sugar, and eggs. Mix well. Stir in cinnamon, vanilla, baking soda, salt, nutmeg, and carrots. Add flour, pineapple, and pecans. Mix well.
3. Pour batter into prepared pan and bake until a toothpick inserted in center comes out clean, 45–50 minutes. Cool in pan. Frost with Cream Cheese Frosting for Best Carrot Cake (recipe follows).

CREAM CHEESE FROSTING FOR BEST CARROT CAKE

YIELD: FROSTING FOR 1 SHEET CAKE

3 ounces cream cheese, softened
1½ cups confectioners' sugar
1 tablespoon unsalted butter, softened
1 teaspoon vanilla extract
¼ cup crushed pineapple, drained
¼ cup finely chopped pecans

In a medium bowl, beat cream cheese with an electric mixer on medium speed. Slowly add the confectioners' sugar, butter, vanilla, and pineapple. Mix well. Stir in pecans. Spread over cooled cake.

DEB'S PINEAPPLE UPSIDE-DOWN CAKE

YIELD: 8–10 SERVINGS

Food historians believe that pineapple upside-down cake has been around since the late 1800s. Some say the first ones were called "skillet cakes." That's because they were often cooked in a skillet on top of the stove instead of in the oven during a time when the traditional method for heating was by wood or coal, which could be very unreliable.

My mother and my sister Debra always baked their pineapple upside-down cakes in the oven, and for the baking pan they used a cast-iron skillet. Not only is it easier to bake the cake in the pan you use to melt the butter, but they often said that baking this cake in a skillet makes the best-tasting cake. I have to agree. This is their version.

½ cup (1 stick) unsalted butter
1 cup brown sugar
1 (20-ounce) can sliced pineapple, drained
10 maraschino cherries, halved
1 cup sifted cake flour
1 teaspoon baking powder
¼ teaspoon salt
4 large eggs, separated
1 cup white sugar
1 tablespoon unsalted butter, melted
1 teaspoon vanilla extract

1. Preheat oven to 325°F. In a 10-inch cast-iron skillet, melt butter over very low heat. Remove from heat and sprinkle brown sugar evenly over butter.
2. Arrange pineapple slices over brown sugar mixture. Place a cherry inside each pineapple hole. Set aside.
3. In a medium bowl, sift together flour, baking powder, and salt. Put the egg whites into a large bowl and beat just until soft peaks form. Gradually add white sugar, beating well after each addition. Beat until stiff peaks form.
4. In a small bowl, beat egg yolks at high speed until very thick and yellow. With a wire whisk or rubber scraper, use an over-and-under motion to gently fold egg yolks and flour mixture into whites. Keep folding until blended. Fold in melted butter and vanilla extract. Spread batter evenly over pineapple in skillet.
5. Bake 30–35 minutes, or until surface springs back when gently pressed with fingertip. Loosen the edges of the cake with a table knife. Cool the cake 10 minutes before inverting onto serving dish. Serve slightly warm.

COCONUT CAKE WITH CREAMY COCONUT FROSTING

1½ cups (3 sticks) unsalted butter, softened
2 cups white sugar
5 large eggs
1½ teaspoons vanilla extract
1½ teaspoons almond extract
3 cups all-purpose flour or 3⅓ cups cake flour
1 teaspoon baking powder
½ teaspoon baking soda
½ teaspoon salt
1¼ cups buttermilk
11 ounces sweetened shredded coconut, divided
Creamy Coconut Frosting (recipe follows)

1. Preheat oven to 350°F. Grease and flour two 9-inch round cake pans. Use cooking spray to grease pans a second time; then lightly dust with flour.
2. In a medium bowl, cream the butter and sugar by beating with electric mixer on medium speed 3 minutes. Add eggs one at a time, beating well after each addition. Add the vanilla and almond extracts. Mix well. Set aside.
3. In a separate bowl, sift together the flour, baking powder, baking soda, and salt. Turn mixer to low speed and then alternate adding dry ingredients and buttermilk to the egg mixture, starting and finishing with dry ingredients. Mix until slightly combined. Stir in 3 ounces coconut.
4. Divide batter between cake pans and level off tops evenly. Bake until cake tested with a toothpick comes out clean, about 40–50 minutes. Cool 15 minutes in pan. Remove layers from pans and cool completely on a rack.
5. Frost the top of the base cake layer with Creamy Coconut Frosting and sprinkle on ¼ cup coconut. Top with remaining layer and spread frosting on top and sides of cake. Sprinkle the top and sides with remaining coconut, press-

ing coconut lightly to blend into the frosting. Refrigerate any leftovers.

CREAMY COCONUT FROSTING

YIELD: FROSTING FOR 1 2-LAYER CAKE

1 (8-ounce) package cream cheese, softened
1 cup (2 sticks) unsalted butter, softened
2 teaspoons vanilla extract
1 pound confectioners' sugar, sifted
3 ounces coconut

In a medium bowl, use an electric mixer on low speed to beat together the cream cheese, butter, and vanilla. Slowly add the confectioners' sugar and beat until blended. Beat only enough to combine; do not overbeat. Stir in coconut and spread on cooled cake layers.

TRADITIONAL RED VELVET CAKE

YIELD: 10–12 SERVINGS

This cake recipe has been in our family for many years. For us, it's always a good choice to serve for special occasions. As a matter of fact, it's a recipe I turn to often for graduation parties, baby showers, and birthdays.

My sister Debra's wedding anniversary and my birthday are only a day apart, so one year we were doing a big joint celebration party at one of the local social clubs in Milwaukee. For this event, I doubled my red velvet recipe and baked it in a half sheet cake pan, which made the cake easy to slice into crowd-friendly squares. Since the cake is red, our party theme was red and white. And the chocolatey-red cake went over well with our guests, who welcomed the change from the traditional birthday cake. Try it for your next celebration.

2¼ cups all-purpose flour
2 teaspoons cocoa
1 teaspoon baking powder
1 teaspoon baking soda
1 teaspoon salt
¾ cup vegetable oil
1½ cups white sugar
2 eggs
1-ounce bottle red food coloring
1 cup buttermilk
1 teaspoon distilled white vinegar
1 teaspoon vanilla extract
Cream Cheese Frosting (recipe follows)

JUICE (WASH) FOR CAKE LAYERS
¾ cup whole milk
½ cup white sugar

1. Preheat oven to 350° F. Grease and flour two 9-inch round baking pans. In a large bowl, sift together flour, cocoa, baking powder, baking soda, and salt. Set aside.
2. In a separate medium bowl, cream together oil and sugar. Add eggs one at a time, beating well after each addition. Add food coloring and mix until well blended. In a separate bowl, combine buttermilk, vinegar, and vanilla. Mix well and add this mixture to oil-sugar mixture, alternating with dry ingredients. Mix well.
3. Spoon batter into pans and bake until center springs back when touched, 25–30 minutes. Cool 5 minutes in pans; then remove from pans and cool completely.
4. Make juice for cake layers: In a small saucepan, combine milk and sugar. Using medium heat and stirring constantly, bring to a boil. Remove from heat and spoon evenly

on top of each cake layer. Let set for 5 minutes before covering with Cream Cheese Frosting.

CREAM CHEESE FROSTING

YIELD: FROSTING FOR 1 2-LAYER CAKE

1 (8-ounce) package cream cheese, softened
½ cup (1 stick) unsalted butter, softened
1 teaspoon vanilla extract
1 pound confectioners' sugar
½ cup chopped pecans
½ cup sweetened, flaked coconut

In a mixing bowl, add cream cheese, butter, and vanilla. Beat with mixer using medium speed until smooth. Gradually add confectioners' sugar while beating using low speed. Mix well. Stir in pecans and coconut. Spread between layers and over cooled cake.

TIP: The juice for the cake layers adds moistness to the entire cake.

OLD-FASHIONED STRAWBERRY CAKE

YIELD: 10–12 SERVINGS

2 cups self-rising flour, sifted
2 cups white sugar
4 large eggs, slightly beaten
1 cup vegetable oil
1 cup whole milk
¼ cup sweetened strawberries, mashed
1 small box (3 ounces) dry strawberry-flavored gelatin

1 teaspoon freshly grated nutmeg
½ teaspoon ground cinnamon
Strawberry Glaze (recipe follows)

1. Preheat oven to 350F. Grease a 9 × 13–inch pan.
2. In a medium bowl, mix flour, sugar, eggs, oil, milk, strawberries, gelatin, nutmeg, and cinnamon. Blend well. Pour
   into greased pan. Bake 25–30 minutes or until a toothpick
   inserted in center comes out clean. Set aside to cool in pan.
3. Spread Strawberry Glaze on cooled cake. Chill in refrigerator at least 2 hours before serving.

STRAWBERRY GLAZE

YIELD: FROSTING FOR 1 SHEET CAKE

4 tablespoons (½ stick) unsalted butter, softened
4 cups confectioners' sugar
⅓ cup sweetened strawberries, mashed
1 teaspoon freshly grated nutmeg

In a large bowl, mix the butter, confectioners' sugar, strawberries, and nutmeg. Blend well. Add more sugar or strawberries if needed for spreading consistency.

ELNORA'S SWEET MILK AND JELLY CAKE

YIELD: 10–12 SERVINGS

*This cake was first introduced to our family many years ago by our good friend
and neighbor Elnora Bell. Elnora brought her recipe with her from Charleston,
South Carolina, and I remember this cake very well because she prepared it on
many occasions. We lived just across the street from Elnora, and, lucky for us,*

she was the type of person who just baked whenever she felt like it; it really didn't have to be for anything special. Elnora is no longer with us, but her daughter and good friend of mine, Carolyn Conley from Ripley, Tennessee, gave me this recipe to include in this chapter.

And this recipe is so simple! The batter is made in one bowl. And the taste of this moist and tender yellow cake sure beats anything that comes out of a box. The glaze is your favorite jelly; it doesn't get any simpler than that. So the next time you want to create memories, try this dessert.

Carolyn Conley shares her memories of this cake: My mother, Elnora Bell, made the best jelly cake in the state of Tennessee. She said that when she did not have any frosting or just didn't feel like making frosting she could always rely on jelly. Placing jelly on a warm cake makes the best cake in the world. My mother brought this recipe from Charleston, South Carolina, her homeland. Enjoy this wonderful cake.

> 1 cup (2 sticks) unsalted butter, softened
> 5 large eggs
> 2 cups white sugar
> 3 cups self-rising flour
> 1 cup whole (sweet) milk
> 1 teaspoon vanilla extract
> 1 teaspoon lemon extract
> 2 cups strawberry jelly (or your favorite flavor)

1. Preheat oven to 350°F. Grease and flour a 9 × 13–inch pan. In a large bowl, use the medium speed of an electric mixer to beat together butter, eggs, and sugar until well-combined, about 2 minutes. Bring mixer speed down to low and beat in flour a little at a time until just combined.
2. Add milk and beat on medium speed until well combined, about 1 minute. Stir in flavorings. Pour batter evenly into the prepared pan.
3. Bake until the center springs back when pressed lightly, 50–60 minutes. Cool 10 minutes. Leave cake in pan and, while it's still warm, spread strawberry jelly over the top. Serve warm or cooled.

HOLIDAY JAM CAKE

YIELD: ABOUT 12 LARGE SERVINGS

My mother made Holiday Jam Cake every year for Christmas, so this cake is strong in my memory of holidays growing up in Halls. Because this recipe is truly special to me, I have never published it. When I misplaced this recipe a few years ago, I was devastated. I just recently found it, so I want to share it with you, and hopefully you can start a holiday tradition.

This is a four-layer cake that calls for a lot of ingredients, and it's best to make it about 5 days before you plan to serve it. Letting the cake set a few days allows the flavors to meld and makes it moist and flavorful. So when the cake is completed, it needs to be wrapped in aluminum foil and then placed in the bottom of the refrigerator—out of sight, out of mind. If not, it will be quickly eaten up.

When my mom made this cake before the holidays, it was hard for my dad to stay out of it. Sometimes on Christmas Eve he would wait until she went to sleep and then sneak into the refrigerator. Even though he knew she frowned upon anyone cutting her cakes before Christmas, he would cut out a huge piece. That would make my mom so mad at him, she would say, "Emerson, you're going to eat the whole cake before Christmas." My dad loved this cake that much.

1 cup solid shortening, preferably nonhydrogenated
2 cups white sugar
4 cups sifted cake flour
1 cup buttermilk
4 whole, large eggs
1 teaspoon baking soda
1 teaspoon ground allspice
1 pinch salt
3 tablespoons cocoa powder
1 cup seedless blackberry jam
1 cup seedless raisins
1 cup chopped pecans
Icing for Holiday Jam Cake (recipe follows)
Mamie's Boiled Custard for serving (recipe
    on page 163)

JUICE FOR HOLIDAY JAM CAKE LAYERS
2½ cups blackberry juice
1 cup white sugar

1. Preheat oven to 350°F. Grease and flour four 9-inch round baking pans.
2. In a large bowl, use medium mixer speed to cream shortening and sugar together, about 3 minutes. Add flour, buttermilk, eggs, baking soda, allspice, salt, and cocoa. Mix until well combined, about 2 minutes. Add jam, raisins, and pecans and blend well.
3. Divide batter among prepared pans. Bake until layers spring back when lightly touched in the center, about 20–25 minutes. Cool 5 minutes. Turn cake layers onto plates and let cool completely.
4. Make juice for cake layers: In a saucepan, bring blackberry juice and sugar to a boil. Stir until sugar is dissolved and remove from heat. Let cool. Brush tops of cake layers with juice and let layers sit 15 minutes.
5. Spread a thin layer of Icing for Holiday Jam Cake between cake layers as you stack them. Pour remaining icing over top and let it run down the sides. (The icing will create a glaze-like texture as it sets.) Once set, wrap in aluminum foil and put in the refrigerator for 3–5 days. Serve on dessert plates over pools of Mamie's Boiled Custard.

ICING FOR HOLIDAY JAM CAKE
4 cups white sugar
1 large can evaporated milk
½ cup (1 stick) unsalted butter
1 cup sweetened coconut
1 cup chopped pecans

In a large pan over medium heat, blend sugar, evaporated milk, and butter. Cook until a ball can be formed when dropped in cold water (soft-ball stage, 235°F). Stir in coconut and chopped pecans. Ice cake while icing is still warm.

MAMIE'S BOILED CUSTARD
YIELD: ABOUT 8–10 (6-OUNCE) SERVINGS

My mother, Mamie, used to make a big bowl of boiled custard for the holidays and serve it in punch glasses alongside her cakes. Sometimes my dad would even pour custard over his plate of cake. I just loved for her to make this at any time of year; it always made a plain cake so special.

2 (12-ounce) cans evaporated milk
2 cups whole milk
8 egg yolks
2 cups white sugar
2 teaspoons vanilla extract
2 teaspoons rum flavor or dark rum
1 teaspoon ground cinnamon, or more to taste
1 teaspoon freshly ground nutmeg, or more to taste

1. In the top of a double boiler over medium heat (see "How to Make a Double Boiler" on page 176), heat the evaporated milk and whole milk until hot but not boiling. Make sure the milk inside the pot is hot.
2. In a separate large bowl, slightly stir egg yolks. Slowly pour hot milk mixture into egg yolks, the whole while stirring slowly. Mix well until blended. Add the sugar; continue to stir. Return milk mixture to double boiler and cook until mixture thickens and coats the back of the spoon, stirring occasionally, for about 35–45 minutes.
3. Remove from heat. Add vanilla, rum flavor, cinnamon, and nutmeg. Stir to blend. Let cool, then cover and refrigerate up to 3 days. Serve warm or cold.

BIG MAMA'S OLD-FASHIONED POUND CAKE

YIELD: 10–12 SERVINGS

Recipes for pound cake first surfaced in eighteenth-century English and American cookbooks. Some of the early pound cake recipes included alcohol and currants, and many were flavored with a hint of lemon. At that time, the pound cake was mostly known as a rich cake that contained a pound of each of the main ingredients: flour, sugar, butter, and fruit; that's how the pound cake got its name.

The pound cake was very popular in the South during the eighteenth century. Today's versions are less rich than they used to be, and there are fewer variations on main ingredients. Even so, it's still served on many of today's southern tables.

Pound cake was Big Mama's favorite cake to bake. When I was a young girl, Big Mama didn't have a mixer, so I used to count with her as she beat the cake batter 300 strokes by hand. The long beating time made the cake batter smooth. She would bake her pound cake in the middle of the week and serve it during that week after we finished dinner.

  1½ cups (3 sticks) unsalted butter, softened
  3 cups white sugar
  1 teaspoon vanilla extract
  1 tablespoon freshly squeezed lemon juice
  8 ounces vanilla yogurt
  1 teaspoon grated lemon rind (zest)
  6 large eggs
  3 cups sifted all-purpose flour
  ½ teaspoon baking powder
  ¼ teaspoon salt
  ½ cup evaporated milk

1. Heat oven to 325°F. Grease and flour a 10-inch tube pan. In a large bowl, use medium mixer speed to beat butter until light and fluffy, about 3 minutes. Add sugar, ½ cup at a time, creaming well after each addition. Stir in vanilla, lemon juice, yogurt, and lemon rind.
2. Add eggs, one at a time, blending well after each addition. In a separate bowl, use a fork to mix together flour, baking

powder, and salt. Add to creamed mixture, alternating with milk and stirring well after each addition. Pour evenly into prepared pan.

3. Bake until wooden pick inserted in center comes out clean, about 60–70 minutes, depending on your oven. Cool 20 minutes, remove from pan.

SOUR CREAM POUND CAKE

YIELD: ABOUT 12 SERVINGS

My older sister, Debra, used to make this cake often. The vanilla extract, along with lemon, adds extra flavor, and the glaze just brings it all together. A wonderful cake to make when company's coming.

3 cups white sugar
1 cup (2 sticks) unsalted butter
6 large eggs, separated
2 teaspoons vanilla extract
1 teaspoon lemon extract
2 tablespoons freshly squeezed lemon juice
1½ cups sour cream
3 cups sifted all-purpose flour
¼ teaspoon baking soda
¼ teaspoon salt
Buttermilk Glaze (recipe follows)

1. Preheat oven to 300°F. Grease and flour a tube pan.
2. In a medium bowl, cream together the sugar and butter for 3 minutes using medium mixer speed. Add egg yolks, one at a time, beating after adding each yolk.
3. Stir in vanilla, lemon extract, lemon juice, and sour cream.
4. In a separate bowl, sift together flour, soda, and salt. Add dry ingredients to batter and beat well, about 2 minutes on medium mixer speed.

5. In a medium bowl, beat the egg whites until stiff peaks form. Gently fold egg white mixture into batter. Mix until blended.

6. Pour batter into prepared pan and bake until cake tester comes out clean, about 1½ hours. Cool in pan 5 minutes. Remove from pan and onto a rack and cool completely.

7. Poke holes on top of the cake with a fork. Pour Buttermilk Glaze over the cake, spread it completely over the top, and let it run down the sides. Before slicing, allow glaze to firm up, about ½ hour.

BUTTERMILK GLAZE
YIELD: ABOUT 1½ CUPS

1 cup white sugar
⅓ cup buttermilk
½ teaspoon baking soda
1 tablespoon white corn syrup
½ cup (1 stick) unsalted butter
1 teaspoon vanilla extract

In a saucepan over medium heat, combine the sugar, buttermilk, baking soda, corn syrup, butter, and vanilla. Bring to a boil, but do not stir until glaze starts to turn dark, after about 5 minutes. The glaze should not reach the soft-ball stage; it should resemble light caramel and be easy to pour.

THREE-FLAVOR POUND CAKE WITH STRAWBERRY RUM TOPPING
YIELD: 10–12 SERVINGS

This was the favorite cake of my Aunt Johnnie Mae from Halls, Tennessee. She called this her "flavor cake" because she would try different flavors, such as brandy, almond, and lemon, or whatever flavor she had on hand. Whatever extract you use, this makes a moist and delicious cake.

½ cup (1 stick) unsalted butter
1 cup (2 sticks) margarine
8 ounces cream cheese, softened
3 cups white sugar
6 large eggs
3 cups sifted cake flour
1 teaspoon ground cinnamon
1 teaspoon freshly grated nutmeg
1 teaspoon vanilla extract
1 teaspoon brandy extract
1 teaspoon lemon extract
8 ounces whole-milk vanilla yogurt
Strawberry Rum Topping (recipe follows)

1. Preheat oven 350°F. Grease and flour a Bundt cake pan.
2. In a large bowl, with an electric mixer on medium speed, cream together butter, margarine, and cream cheese for 3 minutes. Add sugar and continue to cream until light and fluffy, about 2 more minutes. Add eggs one at a time, beating well after each addition. Add flour, cinnamon, nutmeg, and the vanilla, brandy, and lemon extracts. Stir in yogurt. Mix well.
3. Pour batter into prepared pan and bake until a cake tester comes out clean, about 1 hour and 15–20 minutes. Cool 5 minutes in pan before removing. Cool completely before slicing. Top slices with Strawberry Rum Topping.

STRAWBERRY RUM TOPPING

YIELD: ABOUT 3 CUPS

3 tablespoons unsalted butter
¼ cup light brown sugar
2 tablespoons freshly squeezed lemon juice
⅓ cup water
3 medium-sized ripe bananas, peeled and sliced thin

12 fresh strawberries, cut in half

¼ cup light rum (optional)

1. Melt butter in a medium skillet over medium heat. Add brown sugar, lemon juice, and water; stir well. Cook, stirring constantly, until sugar dissolves, 2–3 minutes.
2. Add bananas and strawberries and cook until bananas are soft but not mushy. Remove from heat and stir in rum. Allow to cool 5 minutes. Spoon warm topping over slices of pound cake.

TIP: This topping is great served over ice cream.

SOUTHERN CARAMEL CAKE

YIELD: 10–12 SERVINGS

2 cups self-rising flour

1½ cups white sugar

½ cup (1 stick) unsalted butter, softened

1 cup whole milk

2 medium eggs, unbeaten

1 teaspoon vanilla extract

1 teaspoon lemon extract

½ teaspoon cinnamon

Caramel Frosting (recipe follows)

1. Preheat oven to 375°F. Grease and flour three 9-inch cake pans.
2. In a large bowl, use an electric mixer on medium speed to mix together flour, sugar, butter, and milk. Add eggs, one at a time. Add vanilla and lemon extracts and cinnamon and mix until blended.
3. Pour batter into prepared pans. Bake until centers springs back when lightly touched, 25–30 minutes. Cool 5 minutes in pans. Remove from pans and cool completely. Spread Caramel Frosting between layers and on the cake top and sides.

CARAMEL FROSTING

YIELD: FROSTING FOR 1 3-LAYER CAKE

1 cup (2 sticks) unsalted butter
2 cups light brown sugar
½ cup evaporated milk
1 teaspoon vanilla extract
4 cups confectioners' sugar

1. Melt butter in a saucepan over medium heat. Add brown sugar and milk. Stirring constantly, cook until bubbly and sugar has dissolved completely, 2–3 minutes. Remove from heat and stir in vanilla.
2. Place confectioners' sugar in a large bowl and pour in hot sugar mixture. Beat using medium-low mixer speed until smooth. Let cool slightly before frosting cake.

HUMMINGBIRD CAKE

YIELD: 10–12 SERVINGS

This truly southern cake is thought to have been invented in Jamaica around the 1960s. Its main ingredients, bananas and pineapple, are a complete giveaway of its tropical island origin. Since the cake contains a large amount of fruit, some believe it was named after hummingbirds because it was sweet enough to attract them. However you slice it, the hummingbird cake is different, easy to make, and incredibly delicious.

3 cups sifted all-purpose flour
2 cups white sugar
1 teaspoon salt
1 teaspoon baking soda
1 teaspoon ground cinnamon
3 eggs, beaten
1½ cups vegetable oil

1½ teaspoons vanilla extract

1 (8-ounce) can crushed pineapple, with liquid

2 cups chopped pecans, divided

2 cups mashed ripe bananas

Pineapple Cream Cheese Frosting
   (recipe follows)

1. Preheat oven to 350°F. Grease and flour three 9-inch cake pans. In a large bowl, combine flour, sugar, salt, baking soda, and cinnamon. In a separate bowl, stir together eggs and oil and mix with dry ingredients. Blend until moistened, but do not beat.

2. Stir in vanilla, pineapple and liquid, 1 cup pecans, and bananas. Blend well.

3. Spoon batter into prepared cake pans. Bake until center springs back when touched lightly, about 25–30 minutes. Remove from pans and cool completely. Fill and frost with Pineapple Cream Cheese Frosting. Sprinkle with remaining chopped pecans. Store leftovers in the refrigerator.

PINEAPPLE CREAM CHEESE FROSTING

YIELD: FROSTING FOR 1 3-LAYER CAKE

2 (8-ounce) packages cream cheese, softened

1 cup (2 sticks) unsalted butter, softened

2 (16-ounce) packages confectioners' sugar

1 (8-ounce) can crushed pineapple, with liquid

2 teaspoons vanilla extract

In a large bowl, combine cream cheese and butter. Use medium mixer speed to cream until smooth. Add confectioners' sugar, beating until light and fluffy. Stir in pineapple, pineapple liquid, and vanilla. Immediately spread on cake.

FROSTINGS, ICINGS, AND GLAZES

Cake toppers such as frostings, icings, and glazes add another layer of flavor to any cake. Whether it's a pound cake, or a white, yellow, chocolate, or citrus cake, frosting helps make the cake come alive.

One difference between frosting and icing is that "icing" is the traditional European term, while "frosting" is the word we use in America. Frostings, too, tend to be thicker than icings, and, like buttercream, they have a more fluffy texture, and they often stay soft. Icing, on the other hand, is a little thinner and is more likely to run down the sides of the cake, and when set it has a light shine. Then there are glazes, which are even softer than icing. But don't let a thin layer of glaze fool you—glazes are usually packed with flavor and are therefore delicious poured over your favorite cake.

I think a cake with icing running down the sides is beautiful, and I know that that iced cake will be extra moist. I have to say, however, I prefer cakes with frostings, both for their thick, rich taste and because my mom used frostings a lot in her baking.

The following section has a variety of frostings, sauces, icings, and glazes that can be used however you want. For example, if you're whipping up a yellow cake, you can go with the cream cheese frosting, a glaze, or an icing. The choice is yours. I've also included different toppings that make the right amount for a round cake, a 9×13–inch cake, and pound cakes. And at the end of each recipe, I give tips for the size cakes that that particular topping will frost.

FLUFFY WHITE FROSTING

YIELD: ABOUT 1½ CUPS

1 cup white sugar
⅓ cup water
¼ teaspoon cream of tartar
Dash of salt

2 egg whites
1 teaspoon vanilla extract

1. In a saucepan, combine sugar, water, cream of tartar, and salt. Bring to a boil over medium heat and stir slowly until sugar dissolves.
2. Place eggs whites in medium bowl. Add hot sugar mixture to egg whites and beat constantly with electric mixer until stiff peaks form, about 7 minutes. Beat in vanilla.
3. Spread on cooled cake.

TIP: Can be used for a layered cake, cupcakes, or a 9×13–inch cake.

CARAMEL SAUCE

YIELD: ABOUT 1 CUP

½ cup (1 stick) unsalted butter
1 cup light brown sugar
½ cup heavy cream
1 teaspoon vanilla extract
1 teaspoon ground cinnamon

1. In a skillet over medium heat, melt butter and add sugar. Stir until melted. Add heavy cream. Stir until mixture is smooth and bubbles start to form, about 2 minutes.
2. Remove from heat and stir in vanilla and cinnamon. Cool. Pour over cake or ice cream. Can be stored in refrigerator up to 1 week.

TIP: Pour over a cooled 9×13–inch cake.

PINEAPPLE GLAZE

YIELD: ABOUT 2 CUPS

1 large can (20 ounces) crushed pineapple, with liquid
1 cup white sugar
2 tablespoons unsalted butter, softened
1 teaspoon vanilla extract
1 teaspoon cinnamon

In a medium saucepan over low heat, cook pineapple, sugar, butter, vanilla, and cinnamon until mixture turns slightly syrupy, about 2 minutes. Best if poured hot over a cold cake that was punched with holes while it was still hot.

TIP: Can be used for a cake baked in a 9 × 13–inch pan.

SEVEN-MINUTE FROSTING

YIELD: ABOUT 2 CUPS

Before buttercream frostings became popular, my mother used this frosting for her holiday pineapple and coconut cakes.

2 egg whites
1 pinch salt
1½ cups white sugar
⅓ cup water
¼ teaspoon cream of tartar
1 teaspoon vanilla extract
1 teaspoon coconut extract

1. In a double boiler over medium heat (see "How to Make a Double Boiler" on page 176), add egg whites, salt, sugar,

water, and cream of tartar. Beat over boiling water using a handheld electric mixer on high speed until firm peaks form, about 7 minutes.

2. Remove from heat. Stir in vanilla and coconut extracts. Continue beating with a mixer until frosting is stiff enough to spread. Spread immediately over cooled cake.

TIP: Can be used for a layered cake or a 9×13–inch cake.

CHOCOLATE BUTTERCREAM FROSTING
YIELD: ABOUT 3½ CUPS

This is one of my favorite frostings. With both chocolate and cream cheese, it can't get any better than this.

½ cup (1 stick) unsalted butter
¼ cup unsweetened cocoa powder
1 tablespoon vanilla extract
3½ cups confectioners' sugar
3 ounces cream cheese, softened
4 tablespoons whole milk
½ cup finely chopped pecans (optional)

1. In a saucepan over medium heat, melt butter. Stir in cocoa powder and vanilla. Remove from heat and set aside.
2. In a large bowl, mix confectioners' sugar and cream cheese at low speed. Pour in cocoa mixture and beat well on medium speed. Mixture will be extremely thick. Beat in milk, one tablespoon at a time, until desired consistency is reached.
3. Spread frosting over cooled cake. Add pecans on top, if desired.

TIP: Can be used for a layered cake, cupcakes, or a 9×13–inch cake.

STRAWBERRY BUTTERCREAM FROSTING

YIELD: ABOUT 4 CUPS

½ cup (1 stick) unsalted butter, softened
3 cups confectioners' sugar
1 teaspoon vanilla extract
½ cup fresh strawberries, caps removed and cut in half, with any accumulated liquid
1 teaspoon freshly grated nutmeg
Whole milk (optional)

1. In a mixing bowl with an electric mixer, beat butter until light and fluffy, about 2 minutes. Slowly add the confectioners' sugar and vanilla and beat until smooth.
2. Place strawberries in a blender and puree until smooth. Add pureed strawberries and nutmeg to butter mixture. Continue beating until creamy. If frosting is too thin, add more confectioners' sugar. If too thick, add whole milk, 1 teaspoon at a time, until reaching the desired spreading consistency. Frost cooled cake.

TIP: Can be used for a layered cake, cupcakes, or a 9 × 13–inch cake.

LEMON ICING

YIELD: ABOUT 3½ CUPS

3 cups confectioners' sugar
1½ cups freshly squeezed lemon juice
1 tablespoon unsalted butter, melted

In a medium bowl, use a large spoon to blend together all ingredients until smooth. Pour the icing over a hot cake. Cool before serving.

TIP: Can be used for a pound cake, cupcakes, or a 9 × 13–inch cake.

QUICK RUM GLAZE

YIELD: ABOUT 1 CUP

A quick and wonderful glaze to use during the holidays.

¼ cup whole milk
¾ cup white sugar
2 teaspoons rum flavor or dark rum
½ cup toasted and chopped pecans

Combine all ingredients in a medium bowl. Stir until sugar is dissolved and pour over a warm cake.

TIP: Can be used for a pound cake or a 9 × 13–inch cake.

HOW TO MAKE A DOUBLE BOILER

1. You will need two pots that are different sizes. One pot and a small glass or metal bowl will also work. For the larger pot, use medium heat to heat water that reaches about halfway from the top of the pot. Let water come to a boil.

2. Once water has boiled, place smaller pot or bowl into the larger pot of hot water. The water should not touch the bottom of the smaller pot or bowl.

3. If water in larger pot starts to boil over, you will need to remove some of the water and slightly reduce the heat. Make sure the water in larger pot does not boil over into the mixture.

4. Heat mixture in small, upper pot.

CHAPTER 8

Something Sweet

For many southerners, absolutely no meal is complete without finishing with something sweet. And if my mom cooked a big meal or Sunday dinner and didn't end it with some kind of pastry, we would have asked her if something was wrong. Yes, I love sweets, really more than I care to admit, but I was raised to enjoy dessert.

Sharing family stories, helping Mom in the kitchen, and feasting on homemade sweets pretty much made up my young life. Desserts are a special part of my heritage, as they are throughout the South, and finishing a meal with them still seems like the right thing to do. These sweet endings can come in different shapes, sizes, and colors, and include cookies, brownies, dessert bars, ice creams, and candies. My favorites are old-fashioned, proven desserts, such as cakes, pies, cobblers, and puddings. And if your typical dessert starts from a box or a grocery-store freezer, remember that most Americans are highly seduced by familiar made-from-scratch desserts, those made directly by the hands of home cooks. Don't be afraid to tackle any of it; none of these dishes are time-consuming or hard to put together. And you certainly don't have to go to school to learn how to bake or cook sweets. Most cooks, like me, acquired their skills by simply watching someone they admire in the kitchen. And with all the easy-to-follow dessert recipes out there, satisfying your family's sweet tooth shouldn't be a problem for you, either.

So when did this human urge for something sweet all start? Apparently, our addiction to sweets began in prehistoric times, when honey satisfied cravings. Sugarcane first grew in Southeast Asia thousands of years ago, and it was first granulated in India, reaching the Middle East during medieval times. The Crusaders brought sugar to Europe, where it was expensive and reserved for the wealthy. During the Middle Ages, the rich often enjoyed sophisticated desserts, such as preserved fruits, jellies, gingerbread, and wafers made from a cake-like batter. Marzipan, a thick paste made with almonds and sugar, was introduced into England during this time.

Sugar production back then was extremely labor-intensive. And getting it from the stalk to the table took a sinister turn in the 1400s, when African slaves were being forced to cultivate cane in European-owned islands in the eastern Atlantic Ocean. Then came the European colonization of the Americas and the use of slave labor to work colonial tropical-region cane fields. It wasn't until the 1800s, with the invention of the steam engine, that sugar production became mechanized and efficient, ending the need for a hard-labor workforce.

In the late eighteenth century, German scientists processed sugar from beet roots, and that type of sugar became extremely popular in Europe. Several sweets were introduced during the nineteenth century, including the first chocolate bar and milk chocolate, and the twentieth century saw the birth of many candy bars still popular today. Year after year, more and more sweets were created, and today there are too many treats to count.

I am passionate about baking. And I'm so glad I grew up watching my mother make her signature desserts; this was how my love for baking began at an early age. As time went on, I ventured out and tried new desserts, embellishing them with my own special touches. You, too, can fancy up just about anything homemade with little or no effort just by adding toasted coconut, a scoop of your favorite ice cream, a sprinkling of nuts, or a dollop of whipped cream. And if you want a little something sweet but without much guilt, you can make a fresh fruit bowl and sweeten it with honey.

So whenever you're hit with the desire to have a little fun and stir up candy, freeze ice cream, or bake a new kind of cookie, just remember there are endless treats out there waiting for you to try. And it's easy to turn them into your own famous desserts. All you need is a reliable recipe, a little imagination, and that southern hankering for something sweet.

10 EASY BAKING TIPS TO REMEMBER

1. When baking in a glass dish, reduce oven heat by 25°F.
2. For best results, always bake with eggs and butter at room temperature unless otherwise instructed.
3. Brown sugar will stay soft if you keep it sealed in the refrigerator.
4. Refrigerating chocolate will extend its shelf life.
5. When placing baking pans in the oven, they should never touch each other or be placed over or under each other on the racks.
6. Grease pans using a piece of paper towel. Always grease bottom and sides of the pan with a small amount of shortening, butter, or margarine.
7. When making a new recipe, never guess when measuring ingredients. Use the exact amount that the recipe calls for until you are more familiar with the recipe.
8. Always use fresh ingredients, read labels, and make sure ingredients have not expired.
9. When making a pie crust from scratch, make sure all ingredients are cold.
10. Sweetened condensed milk and evaporated milk are totally different, and one shouldn't be substituted for the other.

SOUTHERN PECAN BARS

YIELD: 15–20 BARS

For me, it's always a good time to try new dessert recipes. But if you want to wait until the holidays and experiment with something other than traditional cakes and pies, pecan bars are a wonderful change. They are an easy alternative to southern pecan pie, and they're so delicious you'll see them disappear right before your eyes. Too, this recipe is simple—a good one for the kids to make on the weekend.

This recipe reminds me so much of growing up in Tennessee, where Big Mama had a large pecan tree on the side of her house. The pecans that came from that tree often ended up in her dessert specialty, homemade pecan pie. This recipe tastes similar to Big Mama's outstanding pie, but it's a lot quicker and easier to make.

1¾ cups all-purpose flour
1⅓ cups firmly packed light brown sugar, divided
¾ cup (1½ sticks) unsalted butter, plus ⅓ cup
　(5⅓ tablespoons) melted butter
3 large eggs
1 cup dark corn syrup
⅛ teaspoon salt
1¼ cups chopped pecans

1. Preheat oven to 350°F. Grease a 9×13–inch baking dish or pan. In a mixing bowl, combine flour and ⅓ cup brown sugar. Cut in ¾ cup butter with pastry blender until mixture resembles coarse meal. Press mixture firmly and evenly into bottom of prepared baking dish. Bake until light brown, 15–18 minutes. Set aside.
2. In a separate bowl, combine remaining 1 cup brown sugar, ⅓ cup melted butter, eggs, corn syrup, and salt; mix well. Stir in pecans. Pour filling over prepared crust. Bake until firm, 35–40 minutes.
3. Let cool completely, and cut into bars. Store in an air-tight container in the refrigerator up to 4 days.

PEANUT BUTTER SQUARES

YIELD: 3 DOZEN SQUARES

½ cup (1 stick) unsalted butter, softened
½ cup packed light brown sugar

1⅓ cups sifted flour
⅔ cup white sugar
⅔ cup light corn syrup
1 (6-ounce) package peanut butter chips
½ cup chunky peanut butter
1½ cups cornflakes

1. Preheat oven to 350°F. In a medium bowl, cream together butter and brown sugar using an electric mixer on medium speed for 3 minutes. Add flour and mix well. Press into the bottom of an ungreased 9 × 13–inch baking dish or pan. Bake 15 minutes. Set aside.
2. In a saucepan, combine white sugar and corn syrup. Bring to a boil over medium heat and remove from heat.
3. Add peanut butter chips and peanut butter, stirring until peanut butter chips melt. Stir in cornflakes. Spread over baked crust, slightly pressing mixture down to even it out. Let cool completely. Cut into squares.

PEANUT BUTTER COOKIES
YIELD: 3½–4 DOZEN

It seems that peanut butter has been a household favorite since the early nineteenth century. Peanut butter cookies are unique in that they traditionally have fork hash marks impressed on top of each cookie. Have you ever wondered why? I sure have, and I learned that these marks were made to alert people who have peanut allergies. The hash marks were introduced in a 1936 Pillsbury cookbook. Nowadays, most people make peanut butter cookies this way simply because we think that's how they're supposed to look. With or without the fork marks, these cookies taste fantastic. Children, in particular, love peanut butter cookies, and they also enjoy making them.

1 cup (2 sticks) unsalted butter, softened
1¼ cups creamy peanut butter

1 cup white sugar

¼ cup light brown sugar

2 eggs

2 cups all-purpose flour, sifted

1 teaspoon baking powder

¼ teaspoon salt

1. Preheat oven to 375°F. In a large bowl, cream butter, peanut butter, and white and brown sugars on medium speed with an electric mixer; beat in eggs. Set aside.
2. In a separate bowl, mix flour, baking powder, and salt. Stir into butter mixture; mix well. Chill dough in refrigerator 1 hour.
3. Roll dough into 1-inch balls and put on baking sheets. Before baking, flatten each ball with a fork; make several crisscross patterns on each ball. Bake until cookies begin to get golden, about 10 minutes. Cool on a rack.

JAM-FILLED CREAM CHEESE COOKIES

YIELD: 30–40 COOKIES

3 ounces cream cheese, softened

1 cup (2 sticks) unsalted butter, softened

2 cups self-rising flour

1 cup white sugar

1 egg yolk

1 teaspoon vanilla extract

Preserves or jam

1. Preheat oven to 350°F. Lightly grease a cookie sheet. In a medium bowl, beat together cream cheese, butter, flour, and sugar on medium speed with an electric mixer until light

and fluffy, about 3 minutes. Beat in egg yolk and vanilla for 1 minute.

2. Drop a tablespoon of dough onto cookie sheet and make a thumb indentation in the center of each cookie. Fill with your favorite preserves or jam (about ½–1 teaspoon per cookie). Bake until edges start to turn brown, 12–15 minutes. Cool on a rack.

LEMON DROP COOKIES

YIELD: 50–60 COOKIES

2 eggs
⅔ cup vegetable oil
1 teaspoon vanilla extract
1 teaspoon lemon extract
1 teaspoon grated lemon peel
¾ cup white sugar
2 cups sifted all-purpose flour
2 teaspoons baking powder
½ teaspoon salt

1. Preheat oven to 400°F. In a medium bowl, beat eggs well with a fork. Stir in oil, vanilla and lemon extracts, and lemon peel. Stir in sugar. Set aside.
2. In a separate bowl, blend together flour, baking powder, and salt. Add flour mixture to the egg mixture and mix until well-combined.
3. Drop dough by the teaspoon 2-inches apart on ungreased cookie sheet.
4. Bake cookies until the edges start to turn brown, about 8–10 minutes. Remove cookies immediately from cookie sheet and let cool.

OATMEAL CHOCOLATE COOKIES

YIELD: 24 SERVINGS

This recipe combines two of my favorite sweet ingredients, condensed milk and chocolate. I love making these cookies, and unfortunately I always find it hard to not overindulge.

1 (14-ounce) can sweetened condensed milk
2 ounces (2 squares) unsweetened chocolate
½ cup chopped pecans
½ cup crunchy peanut butter
1 cup quick-cooking oats

1. Preheat oven to 350°F. Grease a baking sheet. In a double boiler over medium heat (see "How to Make a Double Boiler" on page 176), heat milk and chocolate until mixture melts and thickens, about 6 minutes, stirring occasionally. Remove from heat.
2. To chocolate mixture, stir in pecans, peanut butter, and oats. Mix well. Drop by the teaspoonful onto the greased baking sheet, about 2 inches apart, and bake until set and beginning to dry, about 10–12 minutes. Let cool before serving.

BAKED VANILLA SPICE CUSTARD

YIELD: 6–8 SERVINGS

When all you want is a little something, this is the perfect not-too-sweet dessert. This custard is super-creamy and gets a boost of flavor from cinnamon and nutmeg.

3 large eggs, slightly beaten
¼ cup white sugar

½ teaspoon cinnamon
½ teaspoon freshly grated nutmeg
¼ teaspoon salt
2 cups scalded whole milk, slightly cooled
2 teaspoons vanilla extract

1. Preheat oven to 325°F. In a medium bowl, use a large spoon to beat together eggs, sugar, cinnamon, nutmeg, and salt. Slowly stir in milk and vanilla. Pour into six 5-ounce custard cups or ramekins. Set cups in a pan of hot water, with the water reaching halfway up the outside of the cups.
2. Bake until a knife inserted in the center comes out clean, about 40–45 minutes. Can be served warm or cold.

SWEET POTATO BREAD PUDDING
YIELD: 6–8 SERVINGS

If you love sweet potato pie, you will most definitely love this pudding. And the creamy vanilla sauce just puts it over the top.

4 cups cubed white bread
4 large eggs
3 egg yolks
1 cup whole milk
½ cup evaporated milk
1½ cups heavy cream
1 cup cooked and pureed sweet potatoes
1¼ cups white sugar
¼ cup black seedless raisins (optional)
1 tablespoon rum or brandy
1 teaspoon ground cinnamon
1 teaspoon ground nutmeg

½ teaspoon ground cloves

¼ teaspoon salt

3 tablespoons unsalted butter, cold and cut into
   small pieces

Vanilla Cream Sauce (recipe follows)

1. Preheat oven to 350°F. Grease a 9 × 13–inch baking dish or
   pan. Spread bread cubes on a cookie sheet and bake until
   dry, about 10–15 minutes. Place baked bread cubes in prepared baking dish. Set aside.
2. In a mixing bowl, whisk together eggs, egg yolks, whole
   milk, evaporated milk, heavy cream, sweet potatoes, sugar,
   and raisins. Stir in rum, cinnamon, nutmeg, cloves, and salt.
   Blend well. Pour mixture over bread cubes and let soak until
   mixture is completely absorbed, 5 or more minutes.
3. Dab butter completely over top. Bake until the center of the
   pudding is set but not dry, 30–35 minutes. Serve warm in
   dessert dishes and top with Vanilla Cream Sauce.

VANILLA CREAM SAUCE

YIELD: ABOUT 1½ CUPS

1 (14-ounce) can sweetened condensed milk

1 tablespoon whole milk

1 teaspoon lemon juice

1 teaspoon cinnamon

½ teaspoon ground nutmeg

½ teaspoon vanilla extract

In a small bowl, whisk together all sauce ingredients. Pour
over servings of warm bread pudding and serve immediately. Refrigerate leftovers up to a week.

COCONUT AND RAISIN BREAD PUDDING

YIELD: 10–12 SERVINGS

2 cups water
1½ cups white sugar
1 (12-ounce) can evaporated milk
4 large eggs
1 cup flaked coconut
½ cup crushed pineapple, drained
½ cup seedless raisins
½ cup unsalted butter, melted
1 teaspoon vanilla extract
1 teaspoon ground nutmeg
1 teaspoon ground cinnamon
10 slices white bread with crust, cut
    into ½-inch cubes

1. Preheat oven to 350°F. Grease a 9×13–inch baking dish or
   pan. In a large bowl, combine water and sugar and stir until
   sugar dissolves. Add milk and eggs and whisk until blended.
   Stir in coconut, pineapple, raisins, butter, and vanilla. Blend
   well. Add nutmeg, cinnamon, and bread cubes. Mix well.
   Let mixture stand 35 minutes, stirring occasionally.
2. Pour mixture into prepared dish. Bake until knife inserted
   in center comes out clean, about 45 minutes. Serve warm.
   Refrigerate leftovers.

OLD-FASHIONED STRAWBERRY COBBLER

YIELD: 8–10 SERVINGS

*My cousin Nannie Leake lived in Halls, too, and she used to make this cobbler
often. I still remember going over to visit and watching her take her cobbler out*

of the oven. That luscious scent would fill the house, making it smell like a straw-
berry patch, or as though my cousin was in the middle of canning strawberries.
I just love the memory of those aromas.

 2 (9-inch) unbaked pie crusts
 1½ cups white sugar, plus 1 tablespoon
 ⅓ cup all-purpose flour
 1½ teaspoons ground cinnamon, divided
 1½ teaspoons ground nutmeg, divided
 4 cups fresh sliced strawberries, caps removed
 3 tablespoons unsalted butter, softened
 Whipped Topping (recipe follows)

1. Preheat oven to 375°F. Place one pie crust in a 9×13–inch baking dish or pan, allowing excess dough to fold over pan sides.
2. In a medium bowl, use a large spoon to mix together 1½
   cups sugar, flour, 1 teaspoon cinnamon, and 1 teaspoon nutmeg. Add strawberries; mix just enough to blend.
3. Pour filling into prepared baking dish. Cover with top crust,
   fold excess dough over top, and dot top with butter. Cut
   about 3 slits in top crust; seal the edges.
4. In a small bowl, mix remaining 1 tablespoon sugar, remaining ½ teaspoon cinnamon, and remaining ½ teaspoon nutmeg. Sprinkle on top of crust. Bake until the crust is slightly
   golden, about 35–45 minutes. Cool. When ready to serve,
   top with Whipped Topping. Refrigerate any leftovers.

WHIPPED TOPPING

YIELD: ABOUT 4 CUPS

 3 tablespoons white sugar
 1 (8-ounce) carton cold sour cream
 1 cup cold heavy whipping cream
 ½ teaspoon vanilla extract

1. Make sure bowls and beaters are chilled before using. In a mixing bowl, combine sugar, sour cream, whipping cream, and vanilla. Whip with an electric mixer on high speed until medium peaks form, about 1–2 minutes.
2. Cover and chill in the refrigerator at least 1 hour before serving over Old-Fashioned Strawberry Cobbler.

CLASSIC CHEESECAKE

YIELD: 10–12 SERVINGS

This is one of my very favorite desserts to make. My entire family loves cheesecake, especially my son, Travis. This recipe gets its unique taste from the chopped pecans and ground cinnamon in the crust.

1½ cups graham cracker crumbs (about 10 grahams), divided
⅓ cup finely chopped pecans
⅓ cup white sugar
1 teaspoon ground cinnamon
⅓ cup unsalted butter, melted
2 (8-ounce) packages cream cheese, softened
1 (14-ounce) can sweetened condensed milk
2 large eggs
½ cup freshly squeezed lemon juice
Strawberry Rum Topping (recipe on pages 167–68) (optional)

1. Preheat oven to 325°F. In a small bowl, combine 1 cup cracker crumbs, pecans, sugar, cinnamon, and butter. Mix well. Press the crumb mixture into the bottom and ½ inch up the sides of a 9-inch springform pan. Chill 20 minutes.
2. In a mixing bowl, beat cream cheese on medium speed with an electric mixer until smooth. Add milk, eggs, and lemon juice, and continue beating until completely smooth, about 2 more minutes. Pour over chilled crust.

Sprinkle top with remaining reserved ½ cup crumbs.

3. Bake until center is set, 30–40 minutes. Remove from oven and let cake cool in pan 15 minutes. Gently loosen cake from the edges of pan, but do not remove rim until cooled completely. Chill cheesecake in the refrigerator for 4 hours or overnight. Serve slices topped with Strawberry Rum Topping. Refrigerate leftovers.

TIP: To prevent cheesecake from cracking while baking, insert a pan of hot water on the lower rack of the oven just below the cheesecake. The steam from the water will prevent the cake from cracking.

LEMON TEA CAKES

YIELD: ABOUT 24 CAKES

When I was young, Big Mama used to make these tea cakes right after she took whatever big cake she'd been baking out of the oven. Those little cakes were always packed with big flavor, and the lemon just set it all off. My sister Debra and I couldn't wait for these cakes to get finished baking, and this recipe brings back so many memories and the tradition that Big Mama started.

> 1 cup (2 sticks) unsalted butter
> 1¾ cups white sugar
> 2 large eggs
> 3 cups all-purpose flour
> ½ teaspoon baking powder
> ½ teaspoon salt
> ½ teaspoon baking soda
> 1 teaspoon vanilla extract
> 2 teaspoons lemon extract
> ½ teaspoon ground nutmeg

1. Preheat oven to 325°F. In a medium bowl, cream together the butter and sugar on medium speed of an electric mixer. Beat in eggs, one at a time. Stir in flour, baking powder,

salt, and baking soda. Add vanilla and lemon extracts and nutmeg. Mix well until blended.

2. Knead dough on a floured board until smooth. Form into a flat disk, wrap in plastic, and refrigerate until firm or overnight.

3. Line a cookie sheet with parchment paper. On a lightly floured board, roll dough into a circle about ¼ inch thick. Cut with a 2-inch biscuit or cookie cutter and bake on the prepared cookie sheet until edges turn brown, about 8–10 minutes. Allow cookies to cool 5 minutes on cookie sheet before removing. Serve at room temperature.

STRAWBERRY BUTTER ROLL WITH STRAWBERRY SAUCE

YIELD: 6–8 SERVINGS

Contrary to the sound of its name, a butter roll is not a bread, but an old-fashioned rolled-up pastry dessert, sort of like a stiff jellyroll with a butter and sugar filling. Rumor has it that cooks originally made butter rolls with biscuit or pie scraps. When I was growing up, butter rolls were common throughout the mid-South, and we asked my grandmother to bake them often. (Unfortunately I didn't write down Big Mama's butter roll recipe, but I sure wish I had.) Butter rolls are not traditionally made with any fruit, but since I'm such a big fan of strawberries, I added them to this recipe.

1 pint fresh strawberries, caps removed and berries mashed
1 cup white sugar, plus 2 teaspoons
2 cups all-purpose flour, sifted
1 teaspoon salt
1 teaspoon freshly grated nutmeg
11 tablespoons unsalted butter, softened, divided
1 large egg
⅓ cup whole milk or buttermilk
½ teaspoon cornstarch

1. Preheat oven to 400°F. Grease a cookie sheet or line it with parchment paper. In a small bowl, mix strawberries with 1 cup sugar; set aside.

2. In a medium bowl, sift together flour, salt, and nutmeg. Using a fork, blend in 6 tablespoons butter. Add egg and milk and mix lightly to form a soft dough. Turn out on a floured board and knead to bring dough together. Using flour to keep from dough from sticking, roll out to a 14 × 12–inch rectangle, with long end facing you.

3. Spread 4 tablespoons butter evenly over dough. Strain strawberries, reserving liquid. Spread sweetened strawberries evenly on top of butter. Fold bottom ⅓ of dough up and fold top ⅓ of dough down. Pinch seam to seal and place seamed side down on the prepared cookie sheet.

4. Spread remaining tablespoon butter on top of roll and sprinkle with remaining 2 teaspoons sugar. Bake until golden brown, about 30 minutes. Cool.

5. Meanwhile, place reserved strawberry liquid in a small saucepan and bring to a boil over medium heat. Dissolve cornstarch in a small amount of water and add to pan. Simmer 2 minutes. Remove from heat and cool. Cut the strawberry roll into 2-inch slices and serve over pools of strawberry sauce.

HOLIDAY BRANDY BALLS

YIELD: ABOUT 3½–4 DOZEN

This recipe and the following recipe for Chocolate Nut Cluster Candy are great holiday gifts, and I usually make several batches for the sweet baskets I give family and friends. I remember one Christmas my sister Dawn told me she wasn't into eating sweets, so I only made a sweet basket for my other sister, Debra. But when Dawn tasted the treats from Debra's sweet basket, which included the Brandy Balls and Chocolate Nut Clusters, she put her order in for a sweet basket for the next holiday season.

For more variety in my sweet baskets, I sometimes add assorted homemade cookies and dessert bars. And it's always a good idea to personalize your baskets by including one or two of the lucky recipient's favorite treats. But it never hurts to give them something new to try.

1 (6-ounce) package semi-sweet chocolate morsels
3 tablespoons light corn syrup
½ cup brandy
2½ cups graham cracker crumbs
½ cup confectioners' sugar
1 cup finely chopped pecans
White sugar

1. Melt chocolate in double boiler (see "How to Make a Double Boiler" on page 176). Remove from heat. Blend in corn syrup and brandy. Set aside.
2. In a medium bowl, combine crumbs, confectioners' sugar, and pecans. Add chocolate mixture; mix well. Let stand for 30 minutes.
3. Shape into 1-inch balls, and roll balls in enough white sugar to coat all sides. Let balls season in a covered container for 48 hours before serving.

TIP: You can substitute ½ cup orange juice for the brandy.

CHOCOLATE NUT CLUSTER CANDY

YIELD: ABOUT 2 DOZEN

1 cup milk chocolate chips
1 teaspoon solid shortening, preferably nonhydrogenated
1 cup salted peanuts, divided
1 cup pecan halves, divided

1. Melt chocolate chips with shortening in a double boiler (see "How to Make a Double Boiler" on page 176).

2. To chocolate mixture, add ½ cup of peanuts and ½ cup pecans. Stir until nuts are covered in chocolate.

3. With a fork, remove enough peanuts and pecans from the chocolate mixture to form 1-inch, mounded clusters. Place candy about 2 inches apart on a cookie sheet covered with wax paper.

4. Add remaining ½ cup peanuts and ½ cup pecans to chocolate left in pan. Repeat process. Refrigerate candy until set. Candy can be stored at room temperature up to 2 weeks.

NO-COOK STRAWBERRY OR PEACH ICE CREAM

YIELD: 4 QUARTS

On hot summer weekends, my mother used to churn this old-timey ice cream in a hand-crank freezer packed with salt and ice. Sometimes instead of using strawberries she would make it with freshly peeled and diced peaches. Absolutely delicious! My sister Debra and I always looked forward to this summertime treat.

2 cups white sugar
4 large eggs (Pasteurized eggs are the safest to
    consume raw.)
Dash of salt
1 tablespoon vanilla extract
3 (12-ounce) cans evaporated milk, chilled
2 cups cold whole milk, or as needed
2 cups finely diced fresh strawberries or peeled and
    finely diced fresh peaches
⅔ cup finely chopped pecans (optional)

1. In a large bowl, use an electric mixer at medium speed to cream together sugar and eggs until light and fluffy, about 3 minutes. Stir in salt, vanilla, and evaporated milk. Mix well.

2. Pour mixture into the inside canister of a 4-quart ice cream freezer and add enough whole milk to reach to the

fill line. Add strawberries or peaches and churn according to manufacturer's directions. If desired, top each serving with pecans.

FRESH FRUIT BOWL

YIELD: ABOUT 5–7 CUPS

This cool and refreshing dessert combines fruits and nuts with honey to make a light, sweet treat.

1 cup whole seedless grapes
2 cups peeled and diced cantaloupe
2 cups bite-sized watermelon pieces, seeds removed
1 cup fresh strawberries
1 cup peeled and sliced kiwi
Honey to taste, or 2 tablespoons white sugar
1 cup chopped pecans
1 teaspoon vanilla extract

In a medium bowl, combine grapes, cantaloupe, watermelon, strawberries, and kiwi. Stir together honey, pecans, and vanilla and mix well with fruit. Serve cold. Refrigerate leftovers.

TIP: This recipe is also good with a whipped topping (purchased, or use recipe on pages 188–89).

THE ART OF PIE MAKING

There is something special about making an old-fashioned southern pie. And even though they can look daunting, pies are extremely easy to put together. I also like the fact that they are less expensive to make than traditional homemade cakes.

Pies are historically important to the food of the American South, but they were made in Europe at least as long ago as the early thirteenth century. The word "pie," as it relates to food, was well-known by the year 1362, and back then they were made with or without a crust.

My mom's signature pies were sweet potato, egg custard, and buttermilk. And because everyone loved them, these were the pies that always showed up at funerals, picnics, and family gatherings. For me, the main component of a great pie is the filling. Even if you don't make a homemade crust, a pie can still taste outstanding if you make your own filling. With these recipes anyone—even a child—can make mouthwatering pies with little effort.

MAMA'S PEACH PIE

YIELD: 6–8 SERVINGS

This was one of my mom's favorite recipes. She made it often for Sunday dinner, and she usually had to make at least two for everyone to get a piece. When I was growing up, my Big Mama had two peach trees in her backyard, and she would pick fresh peaches for this recipe. Fortunately, she would usually have some peaches left for canning or just to eat as snacks. I still think homegrown peaches make the best peach pie, so get your hands on some if you can.

>   5 cups peeled and sliced fresh peaches
>   1 cup white sugar, plus 2 tablespoons
>   ½ cup all-purpose flour
>   ½ cup (1 stick) unsalted butter, plus 2 tablespoons,
>   softened
>   3 teaspoons ground cinnamon, divided
>   1 teaspoon ground nutmeg
>   1 teaspoon vanilla extract
>   Pinch of salt
>   2 (9-inch) pie crusts (purchased, or use recipe
>   on page 13)

1. Preheat oven to 350°F. Line a 9-inch pie pan with one pie crust. In a medium saucepan, add peaches, 1 cup sugar, flour, ½ cup butter, 2 teaspoons cinnamon, nutmeg, vanilla, and salt. Stir and cook mixture until slightly thick, 5–10 minutes.
2. Pour mixture into the crust in the pie pan and top with second crust. Cut 3 slits in top crust and seal the edges.
3. In a small bowl, mix the remaining 2 tablespoons sugar and the remaining 1 teaspoon cinnamon. Sprinkle mixture over top crust. Dot with remaining 2 tablespoons butter. Place aluminum foil around the edges to prevent overbrowning.
4. Bake until juice starts bubbling through the slits, about 30–40 minutes. Remove foil during the final 15 minutes of baking. Cool pie to room temperature, 3–4 hours.

LEMON ICEBOX PIE

YIELD: 6–8 SERVINGS

Lemon Icebox Pie is a cousin to the key lime pie and has been a traditional dessert in the South for ages—after all, it seems that lemons have been a favorite ingredient in so much of southern cooking forever. Cookbooks that go back to the seventeenth and eighteenth centuries contain recipes for lemon custards, lemon puddings, pies, and tarts, and food historians tell us that lemon-flavored custards and pies have been enjoyed in Europe since medieval times.

One 9-inch Graham Cracker Crust (use recipe on
    page 198 or purchased)
3 freshly squeezed lemons
2 medium egg yolks
1 teaspoon vanilla extract
1½ (14-ounce) cans sweetened condensed milk
Sour Cream Whipped Topping (recipe follows) (optional)
Thin lemon slices for garnish (optional)

1. Prepare Graham Cracker Crust and set aside.
2. In a bowl, mix together juice from lemons, egg yolks, and vanilla. Gradually stir in condensed milk. Pour into prepared graham cracker crust. Chill pie 2 hours.
3. Serve plain or spread top with Sour Cream Whipped Topping and lemon slices. Refrigerate leftovers.

SOUR CREAM WHIPPED TOPPING
YIELD: ABOUT 1½ cups

½ cup cold heavy cream
½ cup cold sour cream
2 tablespoons confectioners' sugar

In a medium bowl, whip heavy cream, sour cream, and confectioners' sugar with an electric mixer on high speed until medium peaks form, about 1–2 minutes. Use immediately.

GRAHAM CRACKER CRUST
YIELD: ONE 9-INCH CRUST

1½ cups graham cracker crumbs (about 10 whole
   graham crackers)
1 cup unsalted butter, melted
⅓ cup white sugar
1 teaspoon ground cinnamon

1. In a small bowl, use a fork to combine crumbs, butter, sugar, and cinnamon. Use your fingers to press crumbs firmly into the bottom and lower sides of a 9-inch pie plate.
2. Refrigerate until firm, at least 30 minutes, before filling.

TIP: If using whole graham crackers, turn into crumbs in a food processor.

MAMIE'S SWEET POTATO PIE

YIELD: 6–8 SERVINGS

My mother enjoyed making this pie, and my dad absolutely loved it. Mom would make at least four to five sweet potato pies during the holidays, and they always disappeared fast.

1½ cups cooked and mashed sweet potatoes
¾ cup white sugar
¼ cup dark brown sugar
½ cup (1 stick) unsalted butter, softened
2 teaspoons cinnamon
2 teaspoons freshly grated nutmeg
2 large eggs, slightly beaten
1 cup evaporated milk
2 teaspoons vanilla extract
One 9-inch pie crust, unbaked (purchased, or use
   recipe on page 13)
Whipped Topping (recipe on pages 188–89) (optional)

1. Preheat oven to 425°F. In a medium bowl, use an electric mixer on medium speed to beat together sweet potatoes, white sugar, brown sugar, butter, cinnamon, and nutmeg 1 minute.
2. Add eggs, milk, and vanilla. Mix until well blended and smooth.
3. Pour into pie crust and bake 15 minutes. Reduce heat to 350°F and bake until center is set, an additional 30 minutes. Transfer to a rack to cool. Top with whipped topping. Can be made a day ahead. Refrigerate leftovers.

MAMA'S EGG CUSTARD PIE

YIELD: 6–8 SERVINGS

This simple egg custard pie was an absolute favorite in our house. It was the traditional pie my mom made for Easter and Mother's Day, and it was especially expected for the Christmas holidays. My dad loved this pie, and it would not be uncommon for him to eat about half of one at one sitting.

1 (9-inch) unbaked pie crust (purchased, or use recipe
   on page 13)
3 large eggs
1 cup whole milk
3 tablespoons unsalted butter, melted and cooled
⅔ cup white sugar
1 tablespoon all-purpose flour
1 teaspoon cinnamon
½ teaspoon freshly grated nutmeg
1 pinch salt
1 teaspoon vanilla extract

1. Preheat oven to 400°F. Bake crust 8 minutes. Remove from oven and set aside.
2. In a medium bowl, beat eggs on medium speed with an electric mixer for 2 minutes. Add milk, butter, sugar, flour, cinnamon, nutmeg, salt, and vanilla. Mix on medium speed until well blended, about 1 minute.
3. Pour into pie crust and reduce oven temperature to 325°F. Bake until set, 35–45 minutes. Center will still be jiggly, and an inserted knife comes out clean. (Be careful not to over-bake, or the custard will turn watery and the crust will get soggy.) Remove to a rack and cool completely before slicing. Refrigerate leftovers.

CHOCOLATE PECAN PIE

YIELD: 6–8 SERVINGS

Now this is one of my favorite pies to make, and it will satisfy any sweet tooth. I usually reserve it for special events, and it always goes over well with guests. Chocolate Pecan Pie is an extra special treat for pecan pie and chocolate lovers.

3 eggs, slightly beaten

1 cup white sugar

½ cup dark corn syrup

¼ cup (½ stick) unsalted butter, melted

1 teaspoon vanilla extract

⅔ cup chopped pecans

1 (6-ounce) package semi-sweet chocolate chips

1 (9-inch) pie crust, unbaked (purchased, or use recipe on page 13)

1. Preheat oven to 375°F. In a medium bowl, combine eggs, sugar, corn syrup, butter, and vanilla. Mix well. Mix in pecans and chocolate chips.
2. Pour into pie crust and bake until pie is set, 35–40 minutes. Remove to a rack and cool completely. Great served plain or with whipped topping (purchased, or use recipe on pages 188–89).

BUTTERMILK PIE

YIELD: 6–8 SERVINGS

The name may not seem that appealing, but don't let this sweet, sentimental favorite fool you. With its crunchy, slightly burnt sugar top and creamy, custard-like filling, it's always a huge hit.

½ cup unsalted butter

1½ cups white sugar

3 eggs, slightly beaten

¼ cup self-rising cornmeal

½ tablespoon cornstarch

1 tablespoon freshly squeezed lemon juice

1 teaspoon vanilla extract

1 teaspoon freshly grated nutmeg

½ cup buttermilk

1 (9-inch) pie crust, unbaked (purchased, or use
   recipe on page 13)

1. Preheat oven to 350°F. In a medium bowl, use medium speed
   of an electric mixer to cream together butter and sugar for
   2 minutes.
2. Add eggs, cornmeal, cornstarch, and lemon juice. Blend
   well. Add vanilla, nutmeg, and buttermilk, and mix until
   well-blended.
3. Pour into pie crust and bake until pie is set and is lightly
   browned, 30–35 minutes. Let the pie cool on a rack at least
   1 hour. Serve warm or cold. Refrigerate leftovers.

TRADITIONAL APPLE PIE

YIELD: ABOUT 6 SERVINGS

*Apple pies first appeared in cookbooks in America in the eighteenth century, so
this pie certainly is nothing new. But it sure is a favorite that everyone loves. This
version is filled with cinnamon, nutmeg, and allspice. It's good warm or cold, and
it's outstanding topped with a scoop of vanilla ice cream.*

6 cups peeled, cored, and sliced Granny Smith
   or Pippin apples
1 cup white sugar, plus 1 teaspoon
2 tablespoons all-purpose flour
3 teaspoons cinnamon, divided
1 teaspoon nutmeg, freshly grated
½ teaspoon allspice
Dash of salt
2 tablespoons whole milk
2 tablespoons cold butter, cut into small pieces
Two unbaked 9-inch pie crusts (purchased, or
   use recipe on page 13)

1. Preheat oven to 400°F. Fit one pie crust in a 9-inch pie dish.
2. In a medium bowl, stir together apples, 1 cup sugar, flour, 2 teaspoons cinnamon, nutmeg, allspice, and salt. Mix until apples are well coated. Spread apple mixture evenly into first pie crust. Place second pie crust on top of apples. Make sure apples are covered. Press edges together to seal the top crust, and flute the edges with your fingers.
3. Make 3–4 slits into top crust with a knife. Brush top crust with milk. Sprinkle top evenly with remaining 1 teaspoon sugar and remaining 1 teaspoon cinnamon. Scatter 2 tablespoons butter over top of crust. Place pie on a cookie sheet lined with foil to catch drips. Bake until top is golden and juices bubble through slits, 40–45 minutes. Cool at least 30 minutes before serving.

CHAPTER 9

Sitting on the Porch with Sweet Teas and Other Thirst Quenchers

THERE'S nothing like sitting on the front porch on a hot day with your legs propped up on the rocker arms and sipping on an ice-cold glass of sweet tea. Yes, this is definitely a southern tradition, and I was blessed to have grown up with a large, wide front porch to sit on. And there is no doubt that rocking on that porch with a frosty glass in hand somehow makes the tea taste even better.

Our front porch was also the ideal spot for shelling purple-hulled peas and capping fresh strawberries. Too, it was where we listened to Big Mama and our neighbors tell stories about what was happening in the neighborhood; there was no better place to catch up on what was going on in our small town. It seems like only yesterday that I was waving at the neighbors across the street as they went off to work. Oh, what a great time that was. Memories like these are priceless.

Today, we realize that it is a good idea to limit the consumption of sugary drinks. But when you have a thirst that begs to be quenched, not much satisfies more than old-fashioned sweet tea. Here in the South, sweet tea is not just a summertime drink but a year-round staple. In fact, most fast-food restaurants in west Tennessee sell sweet tea by the glass and by the gallon. Yes, by the gallon, because they know that a glass is usually not enough for the average sweet tea drinker.

Strangely to me, sweet tea seems to be peculiar to the South. A few years ago I was dining in a Wisconsin restaurant and ordered sweet tea, and the waitress looked at me with a question mark on her face. We were both highly surprised—she, that there actually was such a thing, and I, because she didn't know what I was talking about.

Tea drinking in America has a long history of being associated with privilege because tea leaves were imported and expensive both before and after the Boston Tea Party. After America's centennial celebration of 1876 in Philadelphia, however, tea's popularity increased. In the early twentieth century, the demand and the love for tea continued and flourished as private teahouses sprung up, giving the average person a place to relax and enjoy a great cup of tea. I would have loved to have been invited to tea in one of those nineteenth-century tea rooms.

Tea is grown on a bush called *camellia sinensis*, and the first tea plant didn't arrive in this country until the late 1700s. Even though we drink a lot of tea in the American South, most of what we consume comes from Asia. South Carolina was the first state to grow tea and the first to produce it commercially, and that state still produces a nice tea.

When we didn't have tea bags to steep and not enough lemons to make lemonade, we always turned to the wide flavor varieties of inexpensive Kool-Aid. That's right, good old Kool-Aid was a big thirst quencher, too, in our house. Kool-Aid is still a big part of southern culinary culture, especially in families with children and for those who need to stretch a budget dollar. I remember after playing outside in the hot sun my mom would open the freezer and pull out Kool-Aid pops she'd made for us, and we would cool off fast. Since we didn't have an air conditioner, we refreshed ourselves with whatever was at hand at the time.

So, regardless of what part of the country you live in, you can create some memories with these beverage recipes, and by sharing stories with family and friends. Oh, and don't forget to wave at the neighbors.

TEA TIPS

1. For perfect tea always start with fresh, filtered cool water or bottled water—never tap water!

2. One reason tea gets cloudy is that hot tea turns that way in the refrigerator. To prevent this from happening, pour steeped tea directly over ice cubes. Also, oversteeping a teabag or squeezing hard on a just-steeped teabag into the tea produces cloudiness.

3. Bitterness in tea happens by overcooking and burning the tea leaves, which can occur when the teabags are steeped too long in boiling water. To help prevent bitterness, add about ⅛ teaspoon of baking soda to the steeped tea after you remove the bags. This method will not affect the taste of the tea.

4. If you use artificial sweetener in your tea, you can use about ¾ cup of sweetener for 2 quarts of steeped tea.

5. If you want additional lemon flavor in your tea, freeze lemonade in ice trays and add the frozen cubes to your glass of tea. As the cubes melt, the lemon flavor will infuse the tea.

SOUTHERN SWEET TEA

YIELD: 2 QUARTS

The southern standard for sweet tea usually starts with ½ cup of sugar for 2 quarts tea. However, if you're not familiar with this great beverage, you can always adjust the sweetness level to your taste. I have read several articles that say southerners love their tea overly sweet. For me, tea is just right when you can taste more tea than sugar. However, many do like it sweeter.

4 cups cool filtered or bottled water, plus additional
5–7 regular-sized tea bags (depending on how strong you like it)
½–1 cup white sugar (or even more!)
¼ cup freshly squeezed lemon juice (optional)

1. In a large saucepan, bring 4 cups water to a rapid boil. Remove from heat; drop in tea bags. Cover and let steep 7–8 minutes.

2. Remove tea bags. Add sugar to hot tea and stir until sugar is dissolved. Pour into a heat-proof pitcher.
3. Add enough cold water to make 2 quarts. Stir in lemon juice. Refrigerate until chilled. Serve over ice.

TIP: First start with ½ cup of sugar then add more to your taste. Just remember that sugar doesn't dissolve well in cold tea.

BIG MAMA'S TEA PUNCH
YIELD: 1 GALLON

7 regular-sized tea bags
1–2 cups white sugar
1 (12-ounce) can frozen orange juice concentrate
1 (12-ounce) can frozen lemonade concentrate
1 (6-ounce) can frozen limeade concentrate
Cold filtered or bottled water

1. Brew tea and stir in sugar according to "Southern Sweet Tea" recipe above. Pour into a 1-gallon container.
2. Add orange juice, lemonade, and limeade. Stir until dissolved.
3. Add enough water to make 1 gallon. Stir until combined. Serve over ice.

ICED PEACH TEA
YIELD: 6 SERVINGS

6 cups cool filtered or bottled water
6 regular-sized tea bags
2 cups freshly peeled and sliced peaches
1 tablespoon fresh mint leaves

½–¾ cup white sugar
Ice cubes

1. In a saucepan, bring water to a rapid boil and remove from heat. Add tea bags and let steep 5 minutes.
2. Add peaches and mint leaves and let set for 5–10 minutes more. Remove tea bags.
3. Pour mixture into a pitcher. Add sugar and stir until sugar is dissolved. Serve cold over ice cubes.

STRAWBERRY ICED SWEET TEA

YIELD: 6 SERVINGS

1 pint fresh strawberries, capped and halved
5 cups chilled brewed sweet tea (recipe on pages 206–207)
½–¾ cup white sugar
¼ cup freshly squeezed lemon juice
Ice cubes

1. Place strawberries in a blender; cover and puree. Pour strawberry puree into a pitcher.
2. Add tea, sugar, and lemon juice. Stir until sugar is dissolved and tea is well blended. Serve over ice cubes.

ICED GREEN TEA

YIELD: ABOUT 5 SERVINGS

Iced green tea is great in the summer; it will cool you off and it is full of healthy antioxidants. According to most dieticians and researchers, both black and green teas have disease-fighting antioxidants, but green tea is especially beneficial. Some researchers also suggest that green tea may help lower choles-terol when you eat a heart-healthy diet, and it can also improve blood vessel and heart health, reduce damage to DNA caused by smoking, and reduce the risk of some cancers. Remarkably, green tea is the second most-consumed beverage in the world, following only water. I like to keep a pitcher of green tea in the refrigerator.

> 5 cups cool filtered or bottled water, divided
> 6 regular-sized green tea bags
> White sugar or no-calorie sweetener, to taste
> Ice cubes

1. In a saucepan, bring 4 cups water to a boil and remove from heat. Add tea bags; cover and steep 5–7 minutes. Once steeped, remove tea bags from water; squeeze gently.
2. Pour tea into a pitcher. Add 1 cup cold water and sweetener to taste. Stir until sweetener fully dissolves. Refrigerate or serve over ice.

SWEET SUN TEA

YIELD: 1 GALLON

This is a great tea the kids can help make. And it's fun watching this tea brew right before your eyes. As children, my sister Debra and I used to sit on the wooden swing in Big Mama's front yard and watch the tea literally brew. The recipe calls for minimal equipment; we would put water and tea bags into a clear glass jar and place it in direct sunlight. We then watched nature take its course. It takes several hours to brew, but it most definitely is worth the wait.

> 5–7 regular-sized tea bags
> 1 gallon cool filtered or bottled water
> ½–1 cup white sugar, or more to taste

1. Select a clean glass container that has a lid; fill with water. Add tea bags, seal with lid. Place sealed jar outside in direct sunlight. Make sure jar is in a protected area. The warmth

from the sun's rays slowly brews the tea, usually in about 4–5 hours, or longer, depending on how strong you want the tea.

2. You will be able to see the tea turn light brown as it brews. Once it is the desired color, remove jar from the sun and remove the tea bags.

3. Add sugar to taste. Stir, then refrigerate, or serve over ice.

SPIKED SWEET TEA

YIELD: 1 PUNCH BOWL

7 cups cool filtered or bottled water, divided
3 tea bags
½ cup loosely packed fresh mint leaves
½ cup white sugar
1 (6-ounce) can frozen lemonade concentrate, thawed
1 cup bourbon or spiced dark rum
Fresh pineapple slices, for garnish

1. In a 2-quart saucepan, bring 3 cups water to a boil. Remove from heat; add tea bags and fresh mint. Cover and steep 7–10 minutes.

2. Once steeped, remove tea bags and strain out mint leaves. Discard mint. Stir in sugar until fully dissolved. Pour tea into a 3-quart punch bowl or food-safe container. Stir in remaining 4 cups cold water and lemonade concentrate.

3. Add bourbon just before serving and mix well. Serve over ice. Garnish with pineapple slices.

OLD-FASHIONED SOUTHERN LEMONADE

YIELD: 8 SERVINGS

My Big Mama made this recipe often, and it was definitely one of her signature thirst quenchers. This is one of those drinks that you pour over a big glass of ice and then sit on the front porch and enjoy. This recipe reminds me so much of growing up, when lemonade was a key drink in our house for any occasion. I remember my mom used to pour her lemonade over ice in a large mason canning jar. Those were the days.

1¾ cups white sugar
½ cup boiling water
2-inch piece lemon peel
1½ cups freshly-squeezed lemon juice
5 cups cold water
Ice cubes
Lemon slices, cut thin

1. In a 2-quart pitcher, add sugar, boiling water, lemon peel, and lemon juice. Stir vigorously until sugar is dissolved. Add cold water. Stir well.
2. Cover and store in refrigerator until ready to serve. Right before serving, add ice cubes and lemon slices. Stir until blended.

STRAWBERRY LEMONADE

YIELD: ABOUT 2½ QUARTS

1 cup fresh strawberries, hulled and cut in half
Cold water
3 cups white sugar, divided
2 cups freshly squeezed lemon juice
Ice cubes for serving
Lemon slices for garnish

1. In a food processor, puree strawberries, 1 cup water, and 1 cup sugar. Set aside.
2. In a large pitcher, add 10 cups cold water, remaining 2 cups sugar, and lemon juice. Add strawberry mixture; stir and taste. Add more sugar if desired. Refrigerate or serve over ice. Garnish with lemon slices.

SWEET TEAS AND OTHER THIRST QUENCHERS

SOUTHERN COMFORT PARTY PUNCH

YIELD: 1 PUNCH BOWL

Even though we have outstanding whiskies in Tennessee, I like making my party punch with a sweet whiskey that originated in New Orleans. In 1894, Southern Comfort liqueur was invented in the famous French Quarter by a bartender named Martin Wilkes "M. W" Heron, who was tired of receiving undrinkable barrels of whiskey from Tennessee and Kentucky. This prompted him to begin working on a recipe to create a whiskey-based drink with a steady quality.

Heron had access to several fruits and many upscale spices that came through the port, such as Moroccan cinnamon and Mexican vanilla. So he began blending these ingredients together to perfect his recipe. He ended up with a whiskey-flavored liqueur that he named "Southern Comfort," and his recipe still remains a big secret. In 1904, Heron's Southern Comfort liqueur was awarded the gold medal for taste and quality at the World's Fair in St. Louis.

I have been making this punch for the holidays for more than 25 years. Even though this recipe calls for a fifth of Southern Comfort, once all the ingredients are mixed together, you'll be surprised at how you really don't recognize how much whiskey is in it. It actually tastes like a fruit punch, and most people want a second and third serving. In fact, a few friends that we seldom see during the year always seem to stop by during the holidays during "punch time." Hmmmm. I wonder why! You have to try this punch to discover what the attraction is.

2 liters 7 Up or Sprite
5 ounces freshly squeezed lime juice
6 ounces frozen concentrated orange juice, thawed
6 ounces frozen concentrated pink lemonade, thawed
1 bottle (a fifth) Southern Comfort
4–5 drops red food coloring, more if needed
4–5 thin orange slices
An ice ring or large ice cubes

1. Make sure all punch ingredients are cold before mixing. In a punch bowl, mix 7 Up, lime juice, orange juice, pink lemonade, and Southern Comfort.

2. Add 2–3 drops of food coloring; mix well. If more food coloring is needed, add a drop at a time until you reach desired color. Stir. Float orange slices on top of punch. Stir in ice and serve immediately in punch glasses.

LEMONADE CRANBERRY COOLER
YIELD: 12 SERVINGS

1 (6-ounce) can frozen lemonade concentrate, thawed
1 (32-ounce) bottle cranberry juice
2 (12-ounce) cans ginger ale, chilled
Ice cubes

1. In a large pitcher, add lemonade, cranberry juice, and ginger ale; stir. Refrigerate.
2. Just before serving, add ice.

WATERMELON CRANBERRY PUNCH
YIELD: 1 PUNCH BOWL

8 cups watermelon chunks, seeded
1 (12-ounce) can frozen cranberry juice concentrate, thawed
1 (6-ounce) can frozen lemonade concentrate, thawed
2 liters ginger ale
Ice ring or large ice cubes

Make sure all ingredients are cold before mixing. In a blender, process watermelon until it turns to juice. Make sure no seeds are in juice. Pour into a punch bowl and add cranberry juice, lemonade, and ginger ale. Mix well. Stir in ice just before serving.

KOOL-AID FRUITY PUNCH

YIELD: 1 PUNCH BOWL

When I was growing up, this was a punch my mom made throughout the summer for all the kids in the neighborhood. This recipe makes a punch bowl full, so it stretched to make a lot of servings.

1 (6-ounce) can frozen orange juice concentrate, thawed
2 packages fruit punch Kool-Aid
2 liters 7 Up
2 cups white sugar
Cold water
Ice cubes

Pour orange juice into punch bowl. Add Kool-Aid, soda, and sugar. If needed, add enough water to fill punch bowl. Mix well. Serve over ice.

KOOL-AID FRUITY POPS

YIELD: 40–45 POPS

1 package Kool-Aid, any flavor
1 cup white sugar
2 quarts water
Juice of ½ freshly squeezed lemon

1. In a large pitcher, mix Kool-Aid, sugar, water, and lemon juice. Mix well.
2. Pour mixture into an ice tray. Tightly cover tray with plastic wrap. When Kool-Aid starts to freeze, insert 2 toothpicks into the center of each cube. Continue freezing until pops are frozen solid.

STRAWBERRY MILKSHAKES

YIELD: ABOUT 4 SERVINGS

1½ cups plain or strawberry yogurt
1 (10-ounce) package frozen and sweetened sliced strawberries
1 cup whole milk
⅔ cup crushed ice
2 tablespoons honey
1 teaspoon vanilla extract
4 fresh strawberries for garnish

1. In a blender on medium speed, combine yogurt, strawberries, milk, ice, honey, and vanilla extract. Cover and blend until mixture is smooth and thick.
2. Pour into chilled glasses. Garnish with strawberries. Serve immediately.

PINEAPPLE SMOOTHIES

YIELD: ABOUT 3 SERVINGS

1 cup whole milk
1 (8-ounce) can sweetened crushed pineapple, with juice
½ cup sweetened pineapple juice
3 tablespoons white sugar
4–5 scoops vanilla ice cream
1 teaspoon vanilla extract
½ teaspoon coconut extract

In a blender, combine milk, crushed pineapple with its juice, pineapple juice, sugar, ice cream, and vanilla and coconut extracts. Cover and blend until smooth. Pour into chilled glasses; serve immediately.

BIBLIOGRAPHY

Avey, Tori. "Where Did Hamburgers Originate?" *Parade Magazine*, August 6, 2013.

"A Brief History of Baking Powder." In *The Cassell's New Universal Cookery Book*. London, 1894. (A recipe for American layer cake appears on page 1031.)

Bryan, Mollie. "The History of Spoon Bread." *Relish*, October 12, 2008.

"Crowder Peas." www.stonofarmmarket.com/crowder-peas.html.

Edelstein, Sari, Bonnie Gerald, Tamara Crutchley Bushell, and Craig Gundersen. *Food and Nutrition at Risk in America: Food Insecurity, Biotechnology, Food Safety, and Bioterrorism*. Burlington, MA: Jones and Bartlett Learning, 2009.

Forman, Mary. "Tea Tips." Deep South Dish website. www.deepsouthdish.com/2008/11/marys-perfect-southern-sweet-iced-tea.html.

Heikenfeld, Rita. "How to Season a Cast Iron Skillet." www.wikihow.com/Season-a-Cast-Iron-Skillet.

"History of Southern Comfort." Cocktail Times website. www.cocktail-times.com/history/southern_comfort.shtml.

"History of Vanilla." *Food History* blog. July 5, 2014. www.world-foodhistory.com/2014/07/history-of-vanilla.html.

"Icing/Frosting." In *Larousse Gastronomique*, revised and updated, p. 617. New York: Clarkson Potter, 2001.

Lambert, Tim. "A Brief History of Sweets." In *An A–Z of Food and Drink*, by John Ayto, p. 254. Oxford: Oxford University Press, 2002.

Laurent, D. "The Joys of Stock." Seeds of Health website. www.seedsofhealth.co.uk/articles/joys_of_stock.shtml.

"Louisiana Sweet Potatoes." Louisiana State University Ag Center Publication 3184. www.lsuagcenter.com/en/communications/publications/publications+catalog/food+and+health/nutrition/louisianasweetpotatoes.htm.

Mariani, John F. *Encyclopedia of American Food and Drink*. New York: Lebhar-Friedman, 1999.

———. "Health Benefits of Cabbage." Nutrition and You website. www.nutrition-and-you.com/cabbage.html.

Moore, Natalie Y. "Buttermilk Pie: An Unexpectedly Sweet Treat." NPR.

February 15, 2006. www.npr.org/templates/story/story.php?storyId=5204275.

Moss, Robert. "The Real Reason Sugar Has No Place in Cornbread." Serious Eats website. August 25, 2014. www.seriouseats.com/2014/08/why-southern-cornbread-shouldnt-have-sugar.html.

Nazario, Brunilda. "Health Tip: Try Tea for a Healthy Resolution." WebMD website. www.webmd.com/diet/health-tip-try-tea-healthy-resolution.

Nelson (Schultz), Jennifer. *Buckets, Bales, and Bushels* blog. https://web.extension.illinois.edu/dmp/eb344/.

Nobles, Cynthia LeJeune. "Summer Cooking on the Grill Can Lead to Debate." *Baton Rouge/New Orleans Advocate*. www.theadvocate.com.

"The Origins of Macaroni and Cheese and Thomas Jefferson." *Eating the World* blog. https://eatingtheworld.wordpress.com/2013/02/19/the-origins-of-macaroni-and-cheese-and-thomas-jefferson/.

Oz, Mehmet. "What Are the Health Benefits of Eating Turkey?" Sharecare website. www.sharecare.com/health/health-value-of-foods/health-benefits-of-eating-turkey.

"Potato History and Fun Facts." United States Potato Board website. www.potatogoodness.com/all-about-potatoes/potato-fun-facts-history/.

Rolek, Barbara. "Definition of Pork or Chicken Cracklings." About Food website. http://easteuropeanfood.about.com/od/ah/g/cracklings.htm.

Stradley, Linda. "History of Hushpuppies." http://whatscookingamerica.net/Bread/Hushpuppies.htm.

Suddath, Claire. "A Brief History of Barbecue." *Time Magazine*, July 3, 2009.

Toussaint-Samat, Maguelonne. *Soups and Stews.* Translated by Anthea Bell. Food Timeline Library. New York: Barnes and Noble, 1992.

Whitaker, Jan. *Tea at the Blue Lantern Inn: A Social History of the Tea Room Craze in America.* New York: St. Martin's Press, 2002.

"Why Local?" 2010 Farm to Table L.L.C. www.farmtotabletx.com/.

Wiggins, Mrs. L. H. "Making the Most of Bananas," *Southern Living*, February 1978, 206.

York, Jake Adam. "Southern BBQ Trail." Southern Foodways Alliance. www.southernfoodways.org.

INDEX OF RECIPES

INDEX OF RECIPES